Lecture Notes in Computer Science 10973

Commenced Publication in 1973
Founding and Former Series Editors:
Gerhard Goos, Juris Hartmanis, and Jan van Leeuwen

Editorial Board

More information about this series at http://www.springer.com/series/7409

Shijun Liu · Bedir Tekinerdogan
Mikio Aoyama · Liang-Jie Zhang (Eds.)

Edge Computing – EDGE 2018

Second International Conference
Held as Part of the Services Conference Federation, SCF 2018
Seattle, WA, USA, June 25–30, 2018
Proceedings

 Springer

Editors
Shijun Liu 🆔
Shandong University
Jinan
China

Bedir Tekinerdogan 🆔
Wageningen University
Wageningen
The Netherlands

Mikio Aoyama
Nanzan University
Nagoya
Japan

Liang-Jie Zhang
Kingdee International Software Group CO., Ltd.
Shenzhen
China

ISSN 0302-9743   ISSN 1611-3349   (electronic)
Lecture Notes in Computer Science
ISBN 978-3-319-94339-8   ISBN 978-3-319-94340-4   (eBook)
https://doi.org/10.1007/978-3-319-94340-4

Library of Congress Control Number: 2018947345

LNCS Sublibrary: SL3 – Information Systems and Applications, incl. Internet/Web, and HCI

Printed on acid-free paper

This Springer imprint is published by the registered company Springer International Publishing AG
part of Springer Nature
The registered company address is: Gewerbestrasse 11, 6330 Cham, Switzerland

Preface

The International Conference on Edge Computing (EDGE) is aimed at becoming a prime international forum for both researchers and industry practitioners to exchange the latest fundamental advances in the state of the art and practice of edge computing, to identify emerging research topics, and to define the future of edge computing.

This volume presents the accepted papers for the 2018 International Conference on Edge Computing (EDGE 2018), held in Seattle, USA, during June 25–30, 2018. EDGE 2018 placed its focus on the state of the art and practice of edge computing, in which topics covered localized resource sharing and connections with the cloud. We accepted 12 papers, including nine full papers and three short papers. Each was reviewed and selected by at least three independent members of the EDGE 2018 international Program Committee. We are pleased to thank the authors whose submissions and participation made this conference possible. We also want to express our thanks to the Organizing Committee and Program Committee members, for their dedication in helping to organize the conference and reviewing the submissions. We owe special thanks to the keynote speakers for their impressive speeches.

May 2018

Shijun Liu
Mikio Aoyama
Bedir Tekinerdogan
Liang-Jie Zhang

Conference Committees

General Chair

Ying Huang   Lenovo, China

Program Chairs

Mikio Aoyama   Nanzan University, Japan
Shijun Liu   Shandong University, China
Bedir Tekinerdogan   Wageningen University, The Netherlands

Application and Industry Track Chairs

Samir Tata   IBM Research, Almaden, USA
Andreas Wombacher   Aurelius Enterprise, The Netherlands

Short Paper Track Chair

Georgia M. Kapitsaki   University of Cyprus, Cyprus

Publicity Chairs

Srividya Bansal   Arizona State University, USA
Shuiguang Deng   Zhejiang University, China

Program Vice Chair

Zhibin Yu   Chinese Academy of Science (Shenzhen), China

Services Conference Federation (SCF 2018)

General Chairs

Wu Chou   Essenlix Corporation, USA
Calton Pu   Georgia Tech, USA

Program Chair

Liang-Jie Zhang   Kingdee International Software Group Co., Ltd, China

Finance Chair

Min Luo   Huawei, USA

Panel Chair

Stephan Reiff-Marganiec   University of Leicester, UK

Tutorial Chair

Carlos A Fonseca   IBM T.J. Watson Research Center, USA

Industry Exhibit and International Affairs Chair

Zhixiong Chen   Mercy College, USA

Operations Committee

Huan Chen (Chair)   Kingdee, China
Jing Zeng   Tsinghua University, China
Yishuang Ning   Tsinghua University, China
Sheng He   Tsinghua University, China
Cheng Li   Tsinghua University, China

Steering Committee

Calton Pu   Georgia Tech, USA
Liang-Jie Zhang (Chair)   Kingdee International Software Group Co., Ltd, China

Program Committee

Haopeng Chen   Shanghai Jiao Tong University, China
Roberto Di Pietro   University of Rome, Italy
Daniel Grosu Grosu   Wayne State University, USA
Jun Han   Swinburne University of Technology, Australia
Mohamad Hoseiny   Sydney University, Australia
Kisung Lee   Luisiana State University, USA
Wei Li   Sydney University, Australia
Wubin Li   Ericsson Research, Italy
Xumin Liu   Rochester Institute of Technology, USA
Min Luo   Huawei, USA
Rui Oliveira   University of Minho, Portugal
Ju Ren   Central South University, China
Han Rui   Chinese Academy of Sciences, China
Rizos Sakellariou   University of Manchester, UK
Jun Shen   University of Wollongong, Australia

Contents

Research Track

Home Edge Computing (HEC): Design of a New Edge Computing Technology for Achieving Ultra-Low Latency

Cheikh Saliou Mbacke Babou[1], Doudou Fall[2(✉)],
Shigeru Kashihara[2], Ibrahima Niang[1], and Youki Kadobayashi[2]

[1] Faculty of Science and Technology,
Cheikh Anta Diop University, 5005 Dakar, Senegal
{cheikhsalioumbacke.babou,
ibrahimal.niang}@ucad.edu.sn
[2] Laboratory for Cyber Resilience, Nara Institute of Science and Technology,
8916-5 Takayama-cho, Ikoma, Nara 630-0192, Japan
{doudou-f,shigeru,youki-k}@is.naist.jp

Abstract. Edge computing systems (Cloudlet, Fog Computing, Multi-access Edge Computing) provide numerous benefits to information technology: reduced latency, improved bandwidth, battery lifetime, etc. Despite all the benefits, edge computing systems have several issues that could significantly reduce the performance of certain applications. Indeed, current edge computing technologies do not assure ultra-low latency for real-time applications and they encounter overloading issues for data processing. To solve the aforementioned issues, we propose Home Edge Computing (HEC): a new three-tier edge computing architecture that provides data storage and processing in close proximity to the users. The term "Home" in Home Edge Computing does not restrain our work to the homes of the users, we take into account other places where the users could connect to the Internet such as: companies, shopping malls, hospitals, etc. Our three-tier architecture is composed of a Home Server, an Edge Server and a Central Cloud which we also find in traditional edge computing architectures. The Home Server is located within the vicinities of the users which allow the achievement of ultra-low latency for applications that could be processed by the said server; this also help reduce the amount of data that could be treated in the Edge Server and the Central Cloud. We demonstrate the validity of our architecture by leveraging the EdgeCloudSim simulation platform. The results of the simulation show that our proposal can, in fact, help achieve ultra-low latency and reduce overloading issues.

Keywords: Home Edge Computing (HEC) · Edge computing systems
Ultra-low latency · Hierarchical architecture · Micro-cells · Three layers

1 Introduction

The main objective of current Edge Computing architectures (Cloudlet, Fog Computing, Multi-access Edge Computing) is to set up a distributed platform for integrating cloud technology into telecommunication networks in order to solve the problems

© Springer International Publishing AG, part of Springer Nature 2018
S. Liu et al. (Eds.): EDGE 2018, LNCS 10973, pp. 3–17, 2018.
https://doi.org/10.1007/978-3-319-94340-4_1

encountered by cloud computing in relation to the emergence of new types of services. But with the advent of the Internet of Things (IoT) [1], hence the increase of the number connected devices that require more real-time processing, current Edge Computing technologies are failing to achieve their goal due to the degradation of the quality of the signal and data overloading at the edge computing level. For instance, if we consider the latest Edge Computing technology, Multi-access Edge Computing (MEC), the above-mentioned issues result in a poor connectivity between the mobile and the base station. This will make the computing capacity at the MEC level significantly reduced along with the performance of the network resulting on technical issues on the user equipment: an increase in power consumption to access the base station which consequently causes a reduction in the life of the batteries. To remedy these problems, a system for stabilizing wireless communication is essential. In addition, the increase in the workload at the system level of the peripheral computing leads to an increase in the service time in the data centers and also a delay in the transmission of the requests in the network which do not meet the requirements of new types of real-time applications. This delay is due to the overload of the communication network where requests from mobile devices converge towards edge computing.

To solve the aforementioned issues, we propose a new concept called Home Edge Computing (HEC), a three-tier edge computing architecture that provides data storage and processing in close proximity to the users. HEC is an extension of MEC, we add another layer of "local data center", namely the Home Server. The latter is located near the user (house, office, company, etc.) but is managed by the Internet Service Provider (ISP). The idea is to implement a miniature cloud in the access point or connection box that a user receives when he/she subscribes to an ISP. In addition to being transparent to the user, we do not need additional infrastructure for the implementation of HEC because this new architecture is based on already existing tools and infrastructures. As a result, requests that are constrained by latency can be processed locally and no longer need to be transferred to the MEC level or the central cloud. We believe that our proposal will contribute to the rapid emergence of 5G by allowing the technologies that are depicted in Fig. 1 to be processed with their required latency and bandwidth. HEC can also help improve the signal strength with the installation of micro-cells at the Home Server level. In order to validate our proposal, we run a simulation by using EdgeCloudSim which is simulation platform for edge computing technologies [16]. The results show that, indeed, Home Edge Computing is better for applications that are latency-sensitive.

The remainder of the paper is structured as follows: we survey the different Edge Cloud technologies in Sect. 2. In Sect. 3, we explain in detail our proposal before validating it through simulation in Sect. 4. Section 5 concludes the paper with a summary and probable future works.

2 Overview of Edge Computing Systems

The set of terms Internet of Things (IoT) was first introduced by Kelvin Aston in a presentation he made at Procter & Gamble (P & G) in 1999 [2]. Gubbi et al. discussed the evolution of wireless technology from Bluetooth to IoT via RFID in parallel with

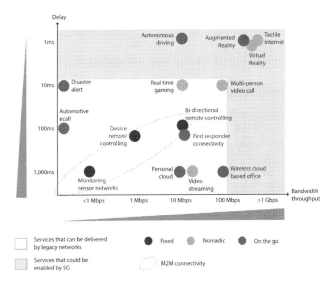

Fig. 1. Bandwidth of latency requirements of potential 5G use cases **Source:** GSMA Intelligence

application domains. They also talked about the achievements and challenges related to IoT in cloud computing technology [2, 3]. In 2019, the majority of data on the Internet will be generated by IoT devices [4] and will be processed at the edge of the network [5]. According to Cisco, by 2020, more than 50 billion objects will be interconnected around the world [6, 21]. As a result, certain types of applications will impose a low latency; others, according to their confidentiality, for example, would need to be processed locally. This is not in sync with the services that cloud computing can offer. Thus, with the many solutions that the edge computing system can offer, players in this area will focus on Edge technologies to address the various problems related to cloud computing technology. In this section, we present a summary of the different architectures of Edge computing systems, their advantages, their limitations and the need for a new Edge computing architecture.

2.1 Concept of Edge Computing Systems

Edge computing systems are introducing new ways to manipulate computing and storage resources. Industry and academia present proposals on the architecture of mobile Edge systems.

Cloudlet. With the advancement of the cloud system and the convergence of new services, mobile users need more resources and accessibility in their environment. As a result, Cloudlet was implemented (Fig. 2(a)). A Cloudlet is a virtualized architecture that spans between mobile devices and a remote cloud, which allows the storage and processing of certain types of data of mobile users without going to the remote cloud. The main goal is to be able to reduce the response time in order to meet the needs of some latency-sensitive applications [13]. Note that the Cloudlet has the advantage of

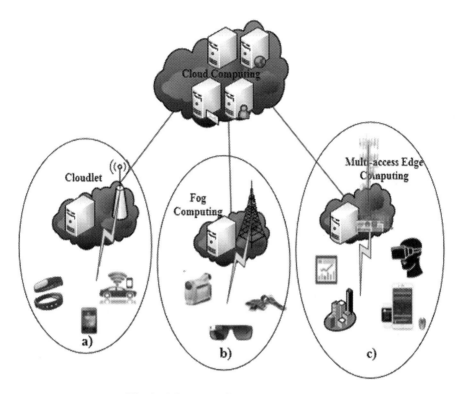

Fig. 2. Edge computing system architectures

being close to the user but does not have the same capabilities as those of the central or remote cloud. Thus its computing capacities are limited for certain services. In addition to its proximity to the users, Cloudlet also has the advantage of being exploited by mobile users who do not even have an internet connection.

Fog Computing. The second architecture of Edge Computing systems is Fog Computing (Fig. 2(b)). The latter extends the services of the central cloud by reducing the amount of data sent to the latter for processing and storage [7]. In addition, Fog Computing system may be integrated into the radio system in the operators' mobile networks [8]. Thus, Fog Computing has the advantages of exploiting storage functions, calculating, controlling, communications between users, depending on the type of requests [9].

Multi-access Edge Computing. The latest concept of Edge Computing systems is Multi-access Edge Computing (MEC). The latter, developed in 2014 by the European Telecommunications Standards Institute (ETSI), enables the provision of resources through cloud servers near users via the Radio Access Network (RAN) tickets [5, 10]. Thus, according to ETSI, MEC allows a considerable reduction of the latency and permits the operators to better locate the positions of the users. Moreover, unlike the aforementioned Edge Computing systems, MEC makes it possible to measure and improve network performance by setting up services (Software Defined Network

(SDN), Network Function Virtualization (NFV), etc.) [12]. Hence, the MEC system has several advantages: availability of the service, reliability, workload. It should be noted that the ultimate goal of MEC is to increase the bandwidth, dramatically reduce the latency and jitter, and provide quality of service (QoS) for mobile applications. MEC is fully integrated into the mobile networks and its servers are located at the base stations. The MEC ecosystem and the integration of MEC servers into the mobile network edge are illustrated in Fig. 2(c), where mobile devices are connected into the base station. The major disadvantage at the MEC level is when its platform is overloaded, there is a poor quality of service performance and an increased latency for real-time services.

2.2 Advantages and Limitations of Edge Computing Systems

Advantages of Edge Computing Systems. Edge computing systems have many advantages over traditional clouds, the most important of which are shown in Table 1.

Limitations of Edge Computing Systems. Despite all the benefits of Edge Computing, there are many drawbacks.

Overload. MEC system failure can occur when a MEC server is overloaded and/or broken. MEC can be overloaded by serving too many tasks, managing too many resources, performing data filtration, or from handling too many service requests [14], as a result, some types of traffic, even those that require minimal physical resources for processing and some that are latency-sensitive, will not be processed in time, which degrades the performance and eventually the quality of service (QoS).

Table 1. Comparison between cloud computing and edge computing systems

Items	CC	MCC	Edge systems
Latency/Jitter	High	High	Low (depends on the rate of use)
Distance to the user	High	High	Low
Deployment	Core network	Core network	Network edge
User devices	Any users	Any users	Mobile users
Storage capacity	Ample	Ample	Limited
Geo-distribution	Internet	Internet	RAN
Architecture	1-tier	1-tier	2-tier
Network access	Any	Any	Mobile
Scalability	Average	High	High
Computational power	Ample	Ample	Limited
Bandwidth saving	No	No	Yes
Battery life time	Limited	Limited	Ample
Utilization of context information	No	No	Yes

Poor signal quality in the macro cells in Edge Computing Systems. For the establishment of the MEC servers, it will first be necessary to make a survey taking into account two main factors the location of sites and areas of high density [14]. In these areas where the traffic is denser, we will have more MEC servers in the same cell (macro cell). On the other hand, this pertinent idea will not solve the problem because certain kind of services will not be satisfied with the performance because of the bad quality of the signal or even the congestion of the base station which is attached to the MEC in question if we take for example Smart Home (in which we have intelligent equipment) [11], it is desirable to bring the computer centers to end users in order to set up microcells in their geographical locations.

2.3 The Need to Propose a New Edge Computing Architecture

Through the limitations of the aforementioned traditional Edge Computing systems and according to the needs of new services such as augmented reality, virtual reality and tactile Internet, the architecture of edge computing system has a critical need to be improved for it to be in phase with these advances. In other words, the requirements of these new applications in terms of proximity, latency and bandwidth cannot be achieved by the current Edge Computing systems. As shown in Fig. 1, the afore-mentioned services require latencies that are between 1 ms and 10 ms and bandwidths that are between 100 Mbps and 1 Gbps. Thus, with the architecture of the current systems of edge computing, this is practically impossible. First, the distance between the user equipment and the base station means that the RTT typically exceeds this latency. In addition, the signal deteriorates as the user equipment moves away from the antenna. This will have consequences on the transmission power of the requests and possibly the bandwidth.

To be able to solve all these problems of Edge computing systems, we propose a new architecture with three levels, called Home Edge Computing (HEC). This new architecture will allow these new services to have a local data center, called Home Server, in which some latency-sensitive requests can be processed. In addition, micro-cells will be integrated into these data centers in order to significantly improve the signal strength and possibly the bandwidth.

3 Home Edge Computing (HEC)

The objective of MEC was to provide Mobile Cloud Computing (MCC) with solutions to the problems that it could not solve such as mobility, response time (for certain types of traffic), proximity, resource optimization, etc. Despite the implementation of MEC in mobile networks, latency is still a major problem, especially if the peripheral system is at its maximum use. In other words, during peak hours (when the traffic has reached its maximum utilization level), there is a congestion at the servers that are found at the edge of the network (it is logical because the resources on the edges of the network are relatively limited). This causes a degradation of the network performance and possibly an increase in response time (latency), even for some requests that require minimum resource for their execution. This situation does not fit the real-time applications:

augmented reality, virtual reality, tactile internet. This will pose a real problem in the future because, according to Cisco, the number of connected objects in the global network continues to increase (the number will triple at the end of 2019, from 15 to 50 billion). In addition, with the establishment of micro-cells at the level of homes, the quality of the signal will be relatively efficient vis-à-vis the macro cells at the level of MEC because the signal on the latter may be very low on some mobiles depending on the distance with the antenna. This will provide a stable signal of good quality allowing fast processing of queries and can save energy. Hence the establishment of a micro-cell at the telecommunication network level is in line with the objectives of the 5G technology which aims to optimize the frequency and the bandwidth; possibly to be able to manage the new generation of intelligent equipment by considerably reducing the latency and also to be able to locally manage certain sensitive data which should not be transmitted all the time to the outside. To overcome these shortcomings, we propose a new architecture called Home Edge Computing (HEC). Our architecture will lighten the work of Multi-access Edge Computing based on certain types of requests by treating them locally.

3.1 What Is Home Edge Computing?

Home Edge Computing (HEC) is a new technique for having a storage and data processing device near the users (Home Server); it also allows us to set up a micro-cell at the user to reduce the workload at the base station located in the MEC and improve system performance. The HEC architecture comprises three levels of cloud (local cloud or Home Server, edge cloud, and central cloud). The term "Home" in Home Edge Computing does not restrain our work to the homes of the users, we take into account other places where the users could connect to the Internet such as: companies, shopping malls, hospitals, etc. Thus, HEC is a new architecture of the edge computing system that is more in proximity to the users compared to Cloudlet, Fog Computing and Multi-access Edge Computing. HEC is a concept proposed to solve the latency problem still present in MEC for certain types of applications that have very high needs in term of resources and have to be processed with relatively reduced delays. With this concept, we will no longer need to go to the MEC or the central cloud for some queries that do not require a lot of computing resources for their processing. One could take the example of smart homes and possibly health care. However, thanks to the synchronization with the edge computing and that of the central cloud, in case of unavailability of the resources on the Home Server, the latter will automatically launch a request, in a hierarchical way, to these two systems which potentially possess resources for satisfying the computational needs of the task.

Thus, several reasons pushed us to create this concept, among which:

- The considerable reduction of the latency (ultra-low latency) for the requests coming from the users equipment and to be able to delegate certain tasks of the MEC server towards the Home Server for the reasons mentioned in [15].
- The installation, at the customer vantage point (office, hospital, company, house, etc.), of a new device relating to the Cloud (Home Server) and a micro-cell that

would alleviate the load of the MEC (and also the eNB) and would be able to satisfy the users in terms performance and processing of certain applications according to their needs in terms of bandwidth and/or latency.

3.2   HEC Architecture

The architecture for Home Edge Computing is depicted in Fig. 3. It is composed of three levels: Home Server, Edge Server and Central Cloud. In the environment of the HEC (home, office, hospital, etc.), all equipment will be wired or wirelessly connected to the local cloud. The Home Server serves, at the same time, as a gateway for this equipment outside the local network because it will be installed and managed by the Internet service provider. Thanks to the proximity of the HEC, the latency-sensitive queries will be rapidly processed. Moreover, for its connection to the rest of the network, we will have to use the system FTTx (Fiber To The x{Home, Office, etc.}) because it has an ultra-low latency and its flow can reach up to 1Gbps, which will correspond to our objective as shown in Fig. 1. Thus, for its operation (Fig. 4), if a request leaves the user's equipment, it is loaded in the box provided by the Internet provider. The Home Server inside the box will handle the customer's request. On this Home server, if the request cannot be processed, the system will hierarchically transfer the request to the cloud (Edge Server or Cloud Central). In addition to lightening the load of the MEC, HEC allows having micro-cells which can also help process latency-sensitive applications. With the Home Edge Computing (HEC) architecture, we can see that the only difference with MEC is the Home Server hosted by the customer. The Home Server has to be tiny, non-cumbersome and transparent to the customer. It must be able to fit within the box that the customer received from the internet service provider i.e. it has to be a mini computer e.g. Raspberry Pi.

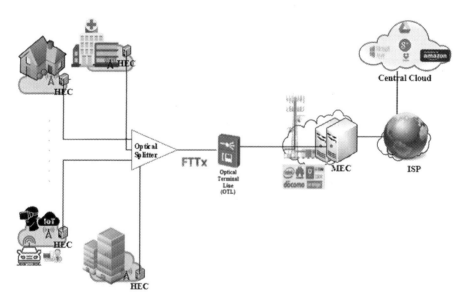

Fig. 3. Home Edge Computing architecture (HEC)

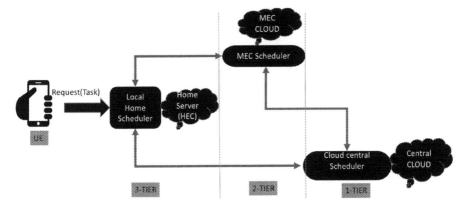

Fig. 4. Processing model in Home Edge Computing (HEC)

Benefits. Home edge computing has many advantages:

- Ultra-low latency for applications that could be treated by the Home Server.
- Reduction of the workload on the Edge Server (MEC).
- Considerable improvement of the signal strength thanks to the installation of micro-cells at each HEC.
- A hierarchical resource allocation system.
- Hierarchical resource allocation: We have what is called the hierarchical aspect at the level of the cloud in general. Thus, any flow from the user (UE, tablet, IoT, laptop, …) will pass the first level i.e. the Home Edge Computing (HEC) will be loaded. If HEC cannot process the request, it will be transferred to the MEC or the Central Cloud. This allows the MEC to have fewer spots (scheduling) and tasks to process.

3.3 Use Cases

In this subsection, we will focus on some of the most specific use cases that experience the need for ultra-low latency for proper operation. As shown in Fig. 1, with respect to our goal and that of 5G technology, we will take the examples of augmented reality, tactile internet and virtual reality. From this fact, we will prove that our proposed solution is more adequate than MEC in terms of latency-sensitive applications.

Augmented Reality. According to Azuma et al. [19], augmented reality can be defined as a system that combines real and computer-generated information in a real-world environment, interactively, in real-time, and aligns virtual objects with physical objects. It is a world in which everything is virtual. In other words, it is closely related to virtual reality. From this fact, the interconnection between the human being and this world can be done by a simple vision, by touch but also by movements. This new concept of HEC will allow the interaction with the real world and that of technology. Moreover, if we talk about this interaction, we think about real-time because nothing can interact with reality without being in phase with it. We can take the example of Daydream View and Google glasses.

Tactile Internet. The term tactile internet was first invented by Prof. Gerhard Fettweis [18]. The tactile internet environment can be considered as a chain environment that includes the touch of the human being (operator) until the task is executed by the robot (remote operator). The architecture of the tactile internet can be divided into three parts, namely the master domain (or of the human), the network domain and the slave domain. Note that communication between the master and the slave is possible thanks to what is called haptic communication, which establishes a link between the human being and the robot through the network domain.

Virtual Reality. The virtual reality system can be defined as the ocular interaction, in real time, between the eye of the human being in general and a 3D representation of the virtual world by the computer according to certain types of software. But this interaction can also involve touch, smell, sound, etc. Thus, to be able to reach this quasi-real concept (approximately $<= 1$ ms for latency), it is necessary to set up a data center very close to the device in question in order to overcome the constraints with regard to network latency and the local processing of these requests from the virtual reality system. Thus, HEC will be better than MEC to meet this challenge as needed in terms of time.

4   Experimental Validation

The main objective of this section is to show the effectiveness of the new HEC compared to MEC. For this, we use the EdgeCloudSim simulator [16] as a simulation environment. This allows us to measure the network latency, the service and the processing time between MEC and HEC.

4.1   EdgeCloudSim

Developed by Sonmez et al. [16], EdgeCloudSim leverages CloudSim [17] to meet the needs of Edge Cloud system specialists. With the CloudSim platform, the specific needs of researchers in the field of mobile edge cloud could not be met. One could even say that EdgeCloudSim is an extension of CloudSim. Because, in addition to having the features of CloudSim, EdgeCloudSim allows offloading tasks to the edge computing. Thus, depending on the needs, different modules are implemented in this environment, namely a mobility module, a load generator module, an edge orchestrator module, a network module and a main management module of the simulation [16]. Note that all these features are based on the CloudSim platform which provides the modules for data centers. In this simulation we focus on the network and data center modules as they relate best to HEC. We need two types of data centers, MEC and HEC. We do not need the Central Cloud in our simulation, because it showed its limits with respect to MEC. So, in a recursive way, we show that HEC has better latency than MEC.

4.2   Simulation Parameters

In our simulation environment, we have to configure 3 types of home devices: the data center, the host and the virtual machine. The configuration of these devices depends on the type of home server we choose. Moreover, in the simulation platform, we have to define different parameters (Tables 2 and 3) and different use cases: virtual reality, augmented reality, tactile internet, gaming. As we show in Fig. 5, in our environment, we consider the two lowest levels: TWO_TIER and THREE_TIER. For the simulation, each scenario (TWO_TIER and THREE_TIER) must be repeated ten times. As a result, 100 new mobile devices are added after each repetition in order to see the evolution of the latency with respect to the WLAN and WAN network respectively at the HEC and MEC positions.

In addition, the majority of configuration parameters (Table 2) are collected from the Cisco Global Mobile Data Traffic Forecast Update [20]. These settings are WAN propagation delay, LAN Internet delay, and bandwidth (for LAN and WAN). The remaining values can be taken at these intervals according to the number of devices and iteration compared to the simulation. Finally, for the orchestration policy, we chose NEXT_FIT because we did not take into account the QoS aspect for this simulation.

Table 2. Default configuration properties

Parameters	Values
Min_num_Dev	[100–1000]
Max_num_Dev	[1000–10000]
Mob_num_Count	[100–1000]
WAN_Prop_Delay (sec)	0.005
LAN_Inter_Delay (sec)	0.1
WAN_Bandwidth (KB)	680
WLAN_Bandwidth (KB)	[1000–10000]
MIPS_For_Cloud	[1000–20000]
Orchestrator_Policies	NEXT_FIT
Simulation_Scenarios	THREE_TIER
	TWO_TIER

Finally, in Table 3, we took the configurations of the Raspberry Pi which will represent our HEC Server. This HEC will allow the hosting of Virtual Machines (VMs) according to requests from User Equipment (UE).

Legend. Min_num_Dev: minimum number of devices, Max_num_Dev: maximum number of devices, Mob_num_Count: mobile devices number count, WAN_-Prop_Delay: WAN propagation delay, LAN_Inter_Delay: LAN internal delay, MIPS_For_Cloud: million instruction per second for cloud.

Table 3. Home devices configuration

	Parameters	Characteristics	Values
Datacenter	Arch.	x86	N/A
	OS	LINUX	
	VM	XEN	
Host	Core	N/A	4
	MIPS		4000
	RAM		2000
	Storage		128000
Virtual machine	VMM	N/A	XEN
	Core		1
	MIPS		1000
	RAM		500
	Storage		10000

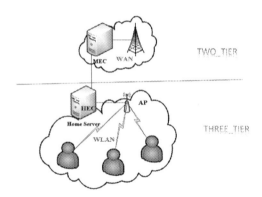

Fig. 5. Simulation architecture in EdgeCLoudSim platform

4.3   Results and Discussion

After the simulation, we could clearly see that it was possible to significantly reduce the latency in the network based on the distance between the two levels (TWO_TIER and THREE_TIER) but also according to the number of mobile devices. Thanks to our method and the help of our simulation platform, we were able to considerably reduce the transmission time of requests using HEC, i.e. the Home Server. Thus, the average delay, under the same conditions, went from 94.82% on the MEC to 5.17% at the HEC level (Fig. 6).

Moreover, as the response time does not depend solely on the network delay, we have also taken into account the service time and the processing time. According to Fig. 6, it was possible to significantly reduce the latency between the MEC and the HEC based on the requests launched by the mobile equipment.

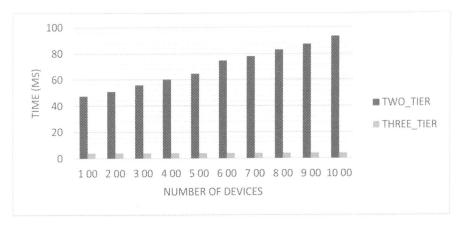

Fig. 6. Network delay

In Fig. 7, we have a visualization of the processing time and the service time of the two data centers: the home server and the edge server. In this figure, we add another y-axis in order to be able to integrate the network delay. Thus, after analysis of the information, we found that, on average, the service and the processing time of the HEC are higher than those of the MEC unlike the situation in Fig. 6. Unsurprisingly, this can easily be explained by the fact that the resources at the MEC level are more important than those of the Home Server according to the MIPS, the number of cores, the RAM, etc.

Our future goal is to find methods or techniques that will allow us to significantly reduce processing and service time.

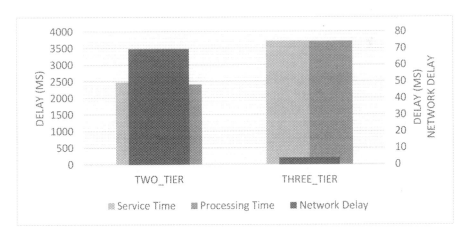

Fig. 7. Latency between HEC and MEC

To remedy these issues, we plan to work on:

- The establishment of a home server cluster that will allow us to distribute the load effectively.
- The implementation of a hierarchical resource allocation system.
- A quality of service policy for real-time services in Home Edge Computing.

5   Conclusion and Future Work

Cloud Computing has been a success in the Information Technology world. But with the advancement of new technologies and the need for mobility, cloud computing has grown rapidly to give birth to Mobile Cloud Computing (MCC). The latter encountered many issues due to constraints imposed by new services and applications. The issues lead to the implementation of the Edge Computing systems (Cloudlet, Fog Computing, Multi-access Edge Computing). With the advent of the IoT, real-time applications, augmented reality services, tactile internet, etc., Edge Computing technologies or the most recent one Multi-access Edge Computing (MEC) faces many difficulties namely the overload of its data centers especially in the peak hours which causes an increase in latency, a degradation of the performance of the applications related to the bad quality of the signal, etc. Hence, to remedy these problems, we proposed a new three-level architecture, called Home Edge Computing (HEC), whose main objective is to significantly reduce latency and to be able to improve the power of the signal by placing micro-cells at the level of each home server. Through simulation, we demonstrated the value of our proposal by reducing the transmission delay between MEC and HEC. For our future work we will focus on the implementation of techniques that will help solve the problems related to the limitation of resources on HEC and we will also focus on resource allocation algorithms in the said edge architecture.

References

1. Twining, J.: Behind the numbers: growth in the Internet of Things. Platform with information from Cisco IBSG (2015)
2. Ashton, K.: That Internet of Things thing. RFiD J. **22**(7), 97–114 (2009)
3. Sundmaeker, H., Guillemin, P., Friess, P., Woelfflé, S.: Vision and challenges for realizing the Internet of things, vol. 20(10) (2010)
4. Cisco global cloud index: forecast and methodology. In: 2014–2019 White Paper (2014)
5. Yi, S., Qin, Z., Li, Q.: Security and privacy issues of fog computing: a survey. In: Xu, K., Zhu, H. (eds.) WASA 2015. LNCS, vol. 9204, pp. 685–695. Springer, Cham (2015). https://doi.org/10.1007/978-3-319-21837-3_67
6. Evans, D.: The Internet of Things: how the next evolution of the Internet is changing everything. In: CISCO White Paper, vol. 1, pp. 1–11 (2011)
7. Chiang, M.: Fog networking: an overview on research opportunities (2016). https://arxiv.org/abs/1601.00835
8. Tandon, R., Simeone, O.: Harnessing cloud and edge synergies: toward an information theory of fog radio access networks. IEEE Commun. Mag. **54**(8), 44–50 (2016)

9. Chiang, M., Zhang, T.: Fog and IoT: an overview of research opportunities. IEEE Internet Things J. **3**(6), 854–864 (2016)
10. Klas, G.I.: Fog computing and mobile edge cloud gain momentum open fog consortium, ETSI MEC and cloudlets. Google Scholar (2015)
11. Rimal, B.P., Van, D.P., Maier, M.: Mobile-edge computing vs. centralized cloud computing in fiber-wireless access networks. In: Proceedings of IEEE Conference on Computer Communication Workshops (INFOCOM WKSHPS), San Francisco, CA, USA, pp. 991–996, April 2016
12. Hu, W., Gao, Y., Ha, K., Wang, J., Amos, B., Chen, Z., Pillai, P., Satyanarayanan, M.: Quantifying the impact of edge computing on mobile applications. In: Proceedings of the 7th ACM SIGOPS Asia-Pacific Workshop on Systems, p. 5. ACM (2016)
13. Gao, Y., Hu, W., Ha, K., Amos, B., Pillai, P., Satyanarayanan, M.: Are cloudlets necessary?" School of Computer Science, Carnegie Mellon University, Pittsburgh, PA, USA, Technical report, CMU-CS-15-139, October 2015
14. Satria, D., Park, D., Jo, M.: Recovery for overloaded mobile edge computing. Future Gener. Comput. Syst. **70**, 138–147 (2017)
15. Mao, Y., You, C., Zhang, J., Huang, K., Letaief, K.B.: Mobile edge computing: survey and research outlook. arXiv preprint arXiv:1701.01090 (2017)
16. Sonmez, C., Ozgovde, A., Ersoy, C.: EdgeCloudSim: an environment for performance evaluation of edge computing systems. In: 2017 Second International Conference on Fog and Mobile Edge Computing (FMEC). IEEE (2017)
17. Buyya, R., Ranjan, R., Calheiros, R.N.: Modeling and simulation of scalable Cloud computing environments and the CloudSim toolkit: challenges and opportunities. In: International Conference on High Performance Computing & Simulation, HPCS 2009. IEEE (2009)
18. Fettweis, G.P.: The tactile internet: applications and challenges. IEEE Veh. Technol. Mag. **9**(1), 64–70 (2014)
19. Azuma, R., Baillot, Y., Behringer, R., Feiner, S., Julier, S., MacIntyre, B.: Recent advances in augmented reality. IEEE Comput. Graph. Appl. **21**(6), 34–47 (2001)
20. https://www.cisco.com/c/en/us/solutions/collateral/service-provider/visual-networking-index-vni/mobile-white-paper-c11-520862.pdf
21. Yamada, M., Cuka, M., Liu, Y., Oda, T., Matsuo, K., Barolli, L.: Design of a smart desk for an IoT Testbed: improving learning efficiency and system security. In: Barolli, L., Enokido, T. (eds.) IMIS 2017. AISC, vol. 612, pp. 27–35. Springer, Cham (2018). https://doi.org/10.1007/978-3-319-61542-4_3

Modular Framework for Data Prefetching and Replacement at the Edge

Dusan Ramljak[1]([✉]) [iD], Deepak Abraham Tom[2], Doug Voigt[3],
and Krishna Kant[1]

[1] Temple University, Philadelphia, PA, USA
{dusan.ramljak,kkant}@temple.edu
[2] University of Florida, Gainesville, FL, USA
deepaktom@ufl.edu
[3] Hewlett Packard Enterprise, Palo Alto, USA
doug.voigt@hpe.com

Abstract. In this paper, we define and evaluate a Bayesian reasoning based cache management framework to minimize data movement and hence the latency and energy consumption of edge devices when interacting with the cloud to retrieve the needed data. The framework can be implemented either directly as a real cache, or as a virtual cache that acts as an advisor to the real cache. The latter strategy is useful when the real cache already exists and deals with complexities such as pinning/unpinning of some objects. The caching framework makes intelligent prefetching and eviction decisions using contextual and temporal relationships while automatically adjusting its parameters in the background. This flexibility and adjustability is crucial for the edge because of the prevalence of the context dependent and heterogeneous nature of the cloud interaction. The paper shows through several storage traces that the mechanism is at least as good as other state of the art algorithms, and can adapt faster to workload changes.

1 Introduction

The increasing proliferation of the Internet of Things (IoT) devices and systems [1–3] results in large amounts of highly heterogeneous data to be collected. It is critical for many of today's organizations to have fast and actionable insight into this data by correlating newly obtained data (at the edge) with the historical or legacy data stored in the cloud. In the resource constrained environment, getting the data that is needed for analysis at the right time is crucial both from application responsiveness and energy consumption perspectives. The edge access patterns are expected to be highly complex and context dependent [4]. This motivates us to study intelligent and flexible caching of the required cloud hosted data at the edge.

Given the importance of context and ability to add any relevant information and address new requirements, Bayesian reasoning provides the opportunity to add evidence (information that will help improve our belief) on the fly. This, in

S. Liu et al. (Eds.): EDGE 2018, LNCS 10973, pp. 18–33, 2018.
https://doi.org/10.1007/978-3-319-94340-4_2

turn, allows us to both adapt to the workload changes and re-train the algorithm to handle new environments.

We use the notion of "belief" to leverage the context of the data. A "belief" encodes relationships across storage entities which could be blocks, objects, files, storage chunks, etc., but generically referred to here as "objects". Consider two objects X and Y and a time window W. The belief of X regarding Y relative to window W, can be defined as the conditional probability that object Y is requested within the time window W following request for X. The belief is then used to determine (or suggest, in case of a virtual cache) the objects to be evicted (low belief) or prefetched (belief higher than elements in the cache, but not present in the cache).

The rest of the paper is organized as follows. Section 2 introduces similarities and differences between our approach and approaches that have been used in related literature to address our needs. The model that we use in the experiments is described in Sect. 3. Data and BeliefCache characteristics are presented in Sect. 4, while results are explained and discussed in Sect. 5. We conclude the paper by providing interesting areas of future studies in Sect. 6.

2   Related Work

Algorithms for predicting future data access in a caching context have been the object of intensive research for many decades at the page, object, cache-line, file, etc. levels, and an enormous body of knowledge has been accumulated in this area. Therefore, we can't provide an extensive survey of cache management and prefetching techniques, just an overview of what we were looking for as a basis for comparison with BeliefCache.

"The cornerstone of read cache management is to keep recently requested data in the cache in the hope that such data will be requested again in the near future [5]". Even though this simple LRU caching and its more complex improvements [6,7] are predictive approaches they rely on the first order caching properties (recency and/or frequency of particular objects) and we wanted to explore them in combination with second order properties (relationships between the objects).

A lot of techniques explore sequentiality since it is important and widely present [8–16]. Yang et al. [17] indicate the need to prefetch based on random access patterns in addition to sequential ones, and observe that a cloud gateway equipped with adaptive caching/prefetching policies could significantly reduce tail latency. There are a lot of methods that leverage the access history information [13,14,18–26]. A lot of them use the weighted edges as a predictor of which objects will be requested next. A possible disadvantage is that rare requests may not be a good enough indicator of what follows next. In our case, we solve this issue by using a window size to allow several requests to vote on what is a likely successor. That way even if the current request is rare, the previous requests can be used to vote for prefetching candidates. Also, in a lot of works prefetching degree and prefetching trigger point are fixed constants throughout the workload. These works [5,8–10,27–30] also try to determine the prefetching trigger point and prefetching degree. In order to be adaptive and flexible we don't fix either, and from request to request, we let the algorithm determine both based on belief. We will show in the experimental section how fixing the prefetching degree affects the quality of the results.

We consider works [17], and it's containing algorithms AMP [5] and SARC [11], as important steps towards augmenting first order caching properties with second order properties, but we aim to go step further. Part of the Tombolo system that prefetches random access patterns is the history based prefetching algorithm they call GRAPH. It works by creating a graph that captures the relationships between requested objects and the requests that occur immediately afterwards. This is an important restriction which affects the ability of GRAPH to address more complex access patterns and adapt to the changes in the workload. We are gauging the relationships between the objects by looking into the window of object successors rather than just the immediate successor. This is a generalization since immediate successor in our framework could be obtained for a window size of 1. We believe that, at the edge, successor relationships are workload dependent. Related objects might come at inconsistent intervals which could be captured by increasing the window of object successors that we are looking into.

Both SARC and AMP, and therefore Tombolo since it is using them, try to relate utility to the amount of space that each part of cache should contain and therefore partly decide which data to keep based on access history. We have a unique policy that is able to address any pattern. Instead of utility, we examine belief and our decisions are related to each object rather than the amount of space necessary for objects in each group.

We rely on the claim from [31] that efficient pattern discovery and description, coupled with the observed predictability of complex patterns within many high-performance applications, offers significant potential to enable many additional I/O optimizations. Thus, we are confident that belief-based caching and prefetching is well grounded and might be a good alternative to address complex access patterns. Directions how to address complex access patterns could also be found in [32].

3   Method

In very broad terms, we rely on the idea of "belief" to guide underlying heuristics in our framework and carry out all of the necessary functions of a cache. Belief is an estimate of a conditional probability that a particular object Y will be accessed next, after accessing X. It is calculated from how many times that object has been accessed in the history "look-ahead" windows matching the current access sequence. Note that the special case of $Y = X$ captures the access recency, and indirectly access frequency of object X. In literature [27,28,33] the "look-ahead" period defines what it means for one file to be opened "soon" after another file. We consider that two files are related if the files are accessed within a "look-ahead" period of one another.

Thus, beliefs provide a directed model of conditional dependence across random access patterns such that integrated use of belief guides both prefetch and eviction decisions. When determining whether a new object should be fetched, we examine the belief we have that it will be accessed in the near future. In order to determine what objects should be removed from the cache, we compare the belief values of the objects currently in the cache and remove the ones with the smallest values. In addition to determining when a new object should be fetched, we also need to decide how many objects should be cycled into the cache. This can range from replacing a single cache element in the event of both a miss and a hit if we believe that another object will be more popular, to replacing multiple objects if we believe that pattern of accesses has been drastically changed. This way we are addressing the increase in complexity of the encountered access patterns.

Maintaining a good hit ratio requires us to constantly monitor and update the belief values of the current cache elements, and compare them against potential replacements to determine if new objects should be cycled into the cache. While maintaining a good hit ratio is important, first priority is to satisfy demand requests as quickly as possible. This is one context where the notion of virtual cache, shown in Fig. 1 becomes important. The vir-

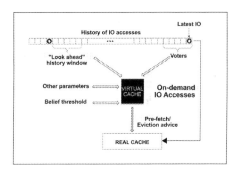

Fig. 1. BeliefCache modular framework

tual cache advises the real cache about the cache objects to be prefetched or evicted based on the belief calculations. This mechanism enables the real cache to service IO access demand requests as fast as possible while the virtual cache (possibly running on a separate core) is doing the belief calculations. Note that the real cache can ignore eviction requests from virtual cache for those objects that need to remain pinned, and can surely ignore prefetch requests if there are too many demand requests to satisfy.

3.1 Calculating Beliefs

For each object we calculate the belief that it will be accessed after the current object if the current object has been accessed more than once. Belief is a conditional probability that an object we are calculating belief for will be accessed in the window of the size h given that we access the current element. Belief for a particular object is calculated as the ratio of the normalized counts of how many times that object appeared in the "look-ahead" history window and counts of how many times that object appeared in any "look-ahead" history window:

$$P(\{x\}|E = o) = \frac{c_{o-x}}{c_{x_p}} \times \frac{f_x}{f_o} \qquad (1)$$

Where $\{x\}$ means that x is in the window of the size h, and $\{x\}|E = o$ therefore means that x is in the window of the size h conditioned that o is the current object. Furthermore, c_{o-x} is the count of x in "look ahead" history windows of o, and c_{x_p} is the count of x in all "look ahead" history windows up to current time and it could be considered as popularity of x. Finally, f_x, f_o are the current overall frequency (could also be considered as credibility of predictive strength) of o, and x respectively.

Moving through the trace we calculate the belief for all objects in the "look-ahead" history window of each object we encounter in the trace.

A rolling history in toy example trace on the left hand side is shown in Fig. 2. Objects are shown by their ids. Circled are the objects for which we count the "look-ahead" history windows. "Look-ahead" history windows of size 5 are represented by rectangles. On the right hand side is how the counts get updated. Counts are updated for the circled objects only when the last object in rectangle is accessed.

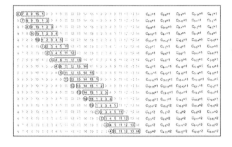

Fig. 2. A rolling history in example trace

For each object we need to keep the counts of only the objects that appear in its "look-ahead" windows. In practice, we update the counts after the fact, when we access the last element in one elements' "look-ahead" window. That is why in the Fig. 2 the last object to have the counts updated is object with the ID 4. Note that Fig. 2 represents overly simplified example trace and look ahead history windows of size 5 and it is shown here for better understanding of the algorithm.

3.2 Virtual Caching Algorithm

Figure 4 gives the virtual caching algorithm which stores the object IDs as well as the sorted beliefs calculated for the current object. As stated before, the virtual cache only determines the belief and what should be prefetched. It does not contain demand request elements unless their ID's are brought in by high belief. We now briefly explain the algorithm with the help of Fig. 3.

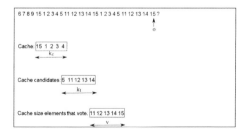

Fig. 3. Cache candidate voting and determination example

Figure 3, shows the trace history of the simple example when a current object o with ID 15 is accessed. Cache represents the objects in the virtual cache (cache size - k_t). Cache candidates (cache candidate size - k_c) are objects that are considered to be put in cache. Cache size elements that vote (vote size - v)

```
 1: function BeliefCache(o)
 2:     Load o
 3:     if c_o > 0 then
 4:         \\Current Beliefs List (BELIEF)
 5:         for All x ≠ o do
 6:             Calculate belief P({x}|E = o)
 7:         end for
 8:         Sort beliefs for x not in cache
 9:         Choose max k_c cache candidates
10:         for x in cache candidates and x in cache do
11:             Find v voters' maximal belief v_max
12:             x_max ← v_max \\x_max is maximum belief
13:         end for
14:         Sort cache candidates and cache elements by maximal belief \\Sorted List
15:         while x_max > threshold and x in Sorted List and x_max > b_s do
16:             Update stored value in BELIEF list
17:             if x not in cache then
18:                 \\Prefetch List (PREFETCH)
19:                 Mark x for prefetching
20:             end if
21:         end while
22:         Suggest objects in PREFETCH list for prefetching
23:         Update beliefs in real cache according to stored BELIEF list
24:     end if
25: end function
```

Fig. 4. BeliefCache virtual cache pseudocode

are objects that vote upon cache candidates and cache elements. All sizes in this toy example, h, v, k_c, and k_t are equal to 5.

For the currently accessed object, "current object" o (line 2), if it has been accessed at least once before (line 3), we first calculate beliefs for all other objects (lines 5–7). Next, we choose k_c objects not currently in the virtual cache which have maximum beliefs that will be accessed after the current object (lines 8–9). We call those objects "cache candidates". We use k_c last accessed elements in the trace, including the current element, to "vote" upon which elements out of the current cache elements and the cache candidates should be in the cache. "Vote" upon means that, for each object in the virtual cache and among the cache candidates, we find the maximum belief that voters provide (lines 10–13).

After obtaining maximal beliefs, we then sort these cache elements and cache candidates according to those maximal beliefs (line 15). Even though we have one sorted list we keep the information which element of the list is cache candidate and which one is already in the virtual cache.

In case of any event, our assumption is that we might need to replace more than one element depending on belief values. Therefore, we try to place in the prefetch suggestion list the top k_c elements from the sorted list of cache candidates and virtual cache elements (lines 15–21). We say "try" because we do so only if, for each object, the obtained maximal belief is higher than the threshold t (line 15). By threshold t we refer to the minimum belief or Bayesian probability required for an object so that it may be considered as a cache candidate. Also, for each element, starting from the top of the sorted list, we compare its found belief value with the smallest stored belief value of the objects in the virtual cache (line 15). If that object from the sorted list was already in the virtual cache we only update its current stored belief value (line 16). If the object from the sorted list was one of the cache candidates we mark it for prefetching from its remote location (line 19), and store its obtained maximal belief (line 16). We continue this process until we reach the list element for which the obtained maximal belief is either smaller than the threshold, or smaller than the smallest stored belief in the virtual cache. After this process is finished, before moving on to consider the next event, we have the list of objects marked for prefetching – PREFETCH (line 22). We update the associated belief values for all objects in the virtual cache based on values from the new object (line 23) and updates for elements we don't want to evict.

Updating the belief for all elements, according to current element beliefs, and updates for the elements we don't want to evict (line 23) prevents building up the high beliefs in the both virtual and real cache. This way we control the ability to effectively change the elements of the real cache.

Subtracting Counts. At equidistant intervals s_l we take a snapshot of the sparse matrix of counts after subtracting the previous snapshot from the current sparse matrix of counts.

Subtracting counts contributes to at least two goals. First, our beliefs remain current and we are able to adapt to workload changes faster. Second, we prevent the overflow of the cells in a sparse matrix of counts which might happen if we experience excessive access to certain elements. Nevertheless, we add a measure to prevent the overflow by limiting the maximal cell number.

Virtual Cache Complexity. Let n be the number of unique objects in the trace. Note, that k_c and h are fixed and lot smaller than n. On the other hand k_w is initially not fixed and is expected to be lot smaller than n.

For each event we have to increment h object counters and h belief counters ($O(h)$ in worst case). We calculate belief and sort k_c best candidates, which takes $O(k_c * log\, k_c * k_w)$. We then sort k_t cache elements with complexity ($O(k_t * log\, k_t)$) and compare at most $2 * k_t(O(k_t))$. The total final complexity could be controlled by avoiding calculation of probabilities when belief could be gauged by simple heuristics, and keeping all lists sorted. In that case each event only costs $O(log\, k_t)$.

The required storage for belief counters is $O(n \times k_w)$. In the worst case scenario, which is highly unlikely, k_w could approach n. In the literature, Oly and Reed [34] claim that can happen only for the most complex, irregular patterns. For that to happen, all objects have to be related to all other objects, or in other words every window after the object needs to contain different objects. Even being so, since h is lot smaller than n and fixed, for all objects to build relationships to other objects they need to be accessed a lot and a lot of time has to pass. However, by subtracting counts we limit the time interval during which this phenomenon would have to occur and therefore k_w could never approach n.

3.3   Real Cache Module

On completion of every IO access virtual cache is supposed to provide the prefetch and eviction advice, i.e. lists PREFETCH and BELIEF. The real cache takes PREFETCH list of elements as an advice for prefetching elements in to itself. For the real cache elements, belief information associated with them is obtained from the belief vector BELIEF which is regularly updated by the virtual cache. However, we keep a copy of the list in case that the list is locked for processing by virtual cache. Additional to this, unlike the virtual cache, the real cache also ensures that the element which it requires to currently access be brought in to the real cache, if the current IO access is a cache miss. For completion, the algorithm for the real cache is shown in Fig. 5

```
 1: function REALCACHE(o)
 2:     Load o
 3:     if PREFETCH and BELIEF not locked then
 4:         Mark elements from PREFETCH for prefetching
 5:         Evict elements with smallest beliefs from BELIEF
 6:     end if
 7:     if cache miss then
 8:         Satisfy demand request
 9:         if BELIEF locked then
10:             Evict elements with smallest beliefs from the stored copy of BELIEF list
11:         else
12:             Evict elements with smallest beliefs from the BELIEF list
13:         end if
14:     end if
15: end function
```

Fig. 5. BeliefCache real cache pseudocode

Note that, since PREFETCH and BELIEF lists are only suggestions real cache could as well use other policies to evict elements.

4   Evaluation Characteristics

In order to show the characteristics of our framework we have built a simulator in which we implemented our algorithm along with algorithms that we intend to compare to, Tombolo (SARC-GRAPH-AMP).

In the following sections we first introduce evaluation measures in Sect. 4.1. Section 4.2 contains the characteristics of the traces we worked with.

Characterization of the effects of user settable parameters, and decisions we made are provided in Sect. 4.3.

All the experiments were performed on 2 6C Intel(R) Xeon(R) CPU E5-2630 v2 @ 2.60 GHz with 128 GB RAM. All code was written in Python 3. Hereinafter, if not stated otherwise for the particular result, all the sizes are relative to the number of unique objects in the trace.

4.1   Evaluation Measures

We consider the following metrics.

(a) Hit ratio: Fraction of requests that have a cache hit over all the requested data (same as fraction of requests that do not incur on-demand fetch latency).
(b) Used ratio: Fraction of objects inserted into cache that receive at least one request before being kicked out.
(c) Insertion ratio (includes prefetch requests and demandfetch requests): Average number of objects inserted per request.

Used ratio is used only to characterize the algorithm in the Sect. 4.3. The important aspects of energy consumption are prefetching and demand fetching. That part of energy consumption is directly proportional to insertion ratio.

4.2   Workloads

We focus on read requests since writes can largely be buffered locally in persistent storage and flushed to remote system asynchronously. We used the trace using only the FileName field to discriminate between what has been accessed, and used TimeStamp, ElapsedTime, and ByteOffset for latency evaluation.

Microsoft Block IO Traces. For our evaluation, we used Microsoft servers block traces, available on the Storage Networking Industry Association (SNIA) website[1]. The traces include Display Ad (DA), Microsoft Network (MSN), and Exchange Server (ES), all collected in 2007-08 time frame.

The traces are primarily Disk IO (block level), File IO traces and represent the original stream of access events already filtered through a cache.

SPEC SFS '14 Workload. The other workload we used is The Video Data Acquisition (VDA), which is a part of SPEC-SFS (a file system benchmark). We set up the cloud gateway file system, cloudfuse, which talks swift API to the Object store and exposes the POSIX interface to the user. As an object store we set up OpenStack on a single node.

The VDA streaming workload is the most appropriate for the edge context since it simulates applications that store data acquired from individual devices such as surveillance camera. Generally, the idea is to admit as many streams as possible subject to bit rate and fidelity constraints. The workload consists of two entities, VDA1 (data stream) and VDA2 (companion applications), each about 36 Mb/s. VDA1 has 100% write access, VDA2 has mostly random read access.

---

[1] http://iotta.snia.org/tracetypes/3.

Workload Characteristics. One of the important characteristics of the workload is object popularity distribution. We calculated it as a CFD (Cumulative Frequency Distribution) of a number of accesses to unique objects arranged in decreasing access rate. Figure 6, shows the object popularity distribution for the DA workload, but all the other popularity distributions look almost the same. x axis represents the fraction of the number of unique objects, while y axis represents the cumulative popularity of the objects. It is seen that relatively small percentage of the number of unique objects is accessed frequently for all traces.

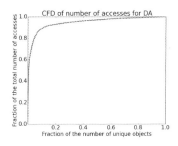

Fig. 6. DA Cumulative freq. dist.

Note that all further evaluations were done for different real cache sizes ranging typically (in terms of number of 16 kB blocks) from 10% to 30% of the number of unique IO accesses in the workload which is less than 3% of the total number of unique objects. The size of the virtual cache was varied between 1 to 100% of the real cache size, as appropriate.

Another important characteristic of the workload is the discretized autocorrelation function. It could show the retention time of objects and is calculated by incrementing a counter each time we encounter the same object being accessed for a given lag value. The function is then plotted after normalization. Figures 7(a), (b), and (c) show the discretized autocorrelation function for the workloads. x axis represents the time lag, while y axis represents the fraction of the number of unique objects that are repeatedly accessed after that lag. For DA it can be seen that the same objects appear regularly with a short gap. MSN workload has very similar characteristics to DA, which is why we are not showing it here. For ES a medium-term "memory" is evident, i.e., a pattern persists for some time and then doesn't show up again. SPEC-SFS shows a truly short pattern and some long term correlations, but they are all rather weak.

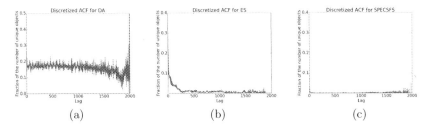

(a)   (b)   (c)

Fig. 7. Discretized autocorrelation for (a) DA, (b) ES, and (c) SPEC SFS

4.3   BeliefCache Characteristics

In this section we discuss BeliefCache characteristics and how internal parameters affect the behaviour of our algorithm. Note that our end goal is to have an adaptive algorithm after the parameters are learned.

General Trends. We noticed that, with the available different workloads exhibiting different short medium and long-term correlations general trends were similar except that peaks and valleys were at slightly different points in the graph.

BeliefCache vs. Fixed Degree Prefetching. BeliefCache, for all of the workloads we measured, significantly outperforms cache management algorithms similar to BeliefCache where the prefetching policy fixes the number of objects to prefetch.

Internal Parameters. The way the parameters are tuned during training is as follows. For each parameter, the value that causes the ratio of hit over insertion to be maximum is chosen. In other words we want our algorithm to provide as good of a hit rate as possible, while keeping the data movement minimal. For the workloads we examined it is sufficient, and algorithm delivers what it promises during the validation.

Parameters are tuned individually so as to reduce the complexity of the training. Tuning the parameters together is possible through the application of randomized optimization algorithm thus finding parameter points that give better results.

Note that, while our algorithm continues to update the probability values during both training and testing, we only learn the values of internal parameters during the training phase.

Training Size: In general there exists a common learning curve for every problem that involves learning. It assumes a low accuracy at the beginning, increase for some period of time and the saturation point. We noticed a lack of common learning curve dependency for Microsoft traces. That could be explained by the fact that our algorithm needs a small amount of data to produce good results, or that for these workloads the amount of training data is not a significant parameter. For SPECSFS trace there is a lot to learn and bigger training sizes are needed.

Cache Candidate Size: Cache candidate size does not affect the virtual cache computation time. However, care must be taken in choosing the appropriate cache candidate size. With an extremely small cache candidate size no significant prefetch takes place. On reaching a suitably high cache candidate size Hit Rate peaks and then remains stagnant with further increase in cache candidate size since what ends up being examined as a cache candidate are the elements with lower belief values.

Voter Size: Contrary to what one would expect the Hit Rate peaks initially and then dips with further increase in voter size. One would expect the prediction accuracy to improve with the increase in number of voters. However, with

increase in the voter size, potentially, the elements with less temporal locality to the current object (further away from it) might boost the belief of the
wrong potential cache candidate element. A large voter size is undesirable since
a larger voter size increases the probability calculation overhead. Therefore, the
best choice of voter size will be a smaller quantity, in fact having a larger voter
size is counter-productive.

Look-ahead History Window Size: With the increase in the window size,
Hit Rate is initially small until a peak is reached. Further on, the trend is again
descending. The reason why this takes place is that, with the increase in the
window size more elements come up in the window of an object and thereby
the probabilities get diluted. As a result, the probabilities do not get to be
sufficiently large in order for the elements to be prefetched in to the cache.
Observing the time for computation with varying look-ahead history window
sizes which steadily increases, it is evident that the best choice of look-ahead
history window size should also be a smaller quantity.

Belief Threshold: As we already mentioned, belief threshold is the minimal
belief that the object should have in order to be considered to be put in the cache.
For the workloads we explored, this parameter proves to have a high value in
protecting the cache from cache pollution. We expect that overprotecting the
cache might hurt the performance.

Hit rate peaks initially and then dips with further increase in belief threshold.
That means we should have a certain belief formed about the objects before we
try to put them in the cache. It is also noticeable that after a certain point
increasing the belief hurts the performance. Lower belief threshold recommends
more irrelevant prefetch elements, which explains the low initial Used Ratio.
With higher belief threshold, the algorithm becomes more conservative about
the elements to be prefetched. This in turn leads to lesser insertions, and thus
directly affecting the Hit Rate.

Tests also showed that the choice of belief threshold does not cause a variation
in the average computation time per IO access in the virtual cache. Thus, the
best choice of belief threshold will be workload specific.

5   BeliefCache Evaluation

Evaluation of the algorithm is done in comparison with Tombolo (SARC-
GRAPH-AMP) in several stages. The most important requirement, the ability
to address complex patterns is addressed first. In Sect. 5.2 we evaluate the speed
of the adjustment. We expect that the framework which better adjusts to the
variations in the workload is better able to reduce the tail latency. Throughout
the experiments both Tombolo and our framework had about the same execution
times.

5.1   Evaluation with Complex Patterns

We compare the performance of BeliefCache against the Tombolo scheme. In
Figs. 8(a), (b), (c), and 9 we show how hit ratio depends on varying the cache

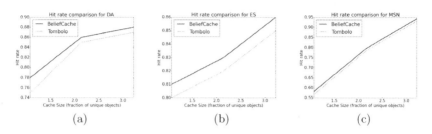

Fig. 8. BeliefCache vs. Tombolo hit rate for (a) DA, (b) ES, & (c) MSN

size. In all figures, x axis represents the cache size as fraction of the number of unique objects and y axis the hit rate. Different line colors represent different prefetching policies. As expected, both algorithms perform better on larger cache on the workloads we examined. For the traces that exhibit random access patterns and short to medium-term correlations it can be seen that BeliefCache is slightly better than Tombolo, but differences are not significant. For the trace which exhibit complex access patterns and long-term correlations BeliefCache is significantly better than Tombolo. Differences could be explained by the decisions to keep the graph manageable and ignore long chains of repeated accesses made in parts of Tombolo that should address the random access patterns.

5.2   Adjustment to the Variations in the Workload

Finally, we evaluate the ability of BeliefCache to adjust to changes in the workload and compare the speed of adjustment to Tombolo.

To do this we have divided traces in two parts. One remains untouched and the other is perturbated. On untouched part we train both algorithms. We measure the hit rate on the perturbated part which is changed on the following way. We kept the same access pattern but changed the objects which exhibit it. For example, if the accesses to objects were 1 7 1 7, we changed it to 2 8 2 8. Therefore, everything that

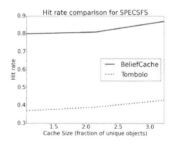

Fig. 9. BeliefCache vs. Tombolo

our algorithm has learned from previous accesses should be changed to adjust to perturbation. Since the access patterns remain the same, both algorithms should at some point recover the measured hit rate on that part before the perturbation.

For all the examined workloads BeliefCache recovers the previous hit rate 2 times faster than Tombolo. As the experiment shows BeliefCache quickly adopts to the new workload and converges to the old hit rate result, requiring only a small fraction of the new test set to make the adjustment. On the other hand Tombolo's prefetching has a slight upward slope as it is going through the trace. This implies a rigidity of the structure that is being created as part of the relationship it has created between different objects in the trace.

6   Conclusions and Future Work

The BeliefCache modular framework exploits contextual and temporal relationships gauged from the access history in the presence of complex access patterns at the edge to improve prefetching and eviction performance. In this work – time window, voting window size and belief threshold are among the parameters learned from access history and kept constant while executing the framework. In contrast, the beliefs themselves are dynamic values that are updated on each request. The elements with the highest belief values are considered for prefetching and those with the lowest values for eviction. The net result is a unified prefetching/caching algorithm that is not only competitive with the state-of-the-art algorithms, but can also quickly adjust itself to changes in workload.

Important next steps are to explore the robustness of the parameters with respect to the workload changes. Clearly, if the workload changes very substantially, the performance of the algorithm may drop and require an update to the parameters. Understanding the right time when to retrain the parameters might improve the performance of the framework. Further, interesting avenues of research would be to extend the belief by looking at temporal, behavioral and structural factors and explore multiple sets of beliefs.

Acknowledgments. The authors would like to thank Sam Fineberg, and other colleagues from HPE, Jesse Friedman, Anis Alazzawe, and Alexey Uversky from Temple University, for valuable discussions and contributions in the initial phases of this work.

References

1. Gubbi, J., et al.: Internet of things (IoT): a vision, architectural elements, and future directions. Future Gener. Comput. Syst. **29**(7), 1645–1660 (2013)
2. Rose, K., et al.: The Internet of Things: An Overview. The Internet Society
3. Kolb, S., Lenhard, J., Wirtz, G.: Application migration effort in the cloud. Serv. Trans. Cloud Comput. **3**(4), 1–15 (2015)
4. Zhang, F., et al.: Edgebuffer: caching and prefetching content at the edge in the mobility first future internet architecture. In: 2015 IEEE 16th International Symposium on World of Wireless, Mobile and Multimedia Networks (WoWMoM), pp. 1–9. IEEE (2015)
5. Gill, B.S., Bathen, L.A.D.: AMP: adaptive multi-stream prefetching in a shared cache. In: FAST, vol. 7, pp. 185–198 (2007)
6. Arı, İ., et al.: ACME: adaptive caching using multiple experts. In: Proceedings in Informatics, vol. 14 (2002)
7. Megiddo, N., Modha, D.S.: ARC: a self-tuning, low overhead replacement cache. In: FAST, vol. 3, pp. 115–130 (2003)
8. Smith, A.J.: Cache memories. ACM Comput. Surv. (CSUR) **14**(3), 473–530 (1982)
9. Tcheun, M.K., et al.: An adaptive sequential prefetching scheme in shared-memory multiprocessors. In: Proceedings of the 1997 International Conference on Parallel Processing, pp. 306–313. IEEE (1997)
10. Pendse, R., Bhagavathula, R.: Pre-fetching with the segmented LRU algorithm. In: 42nd Midwest Symposium on Circuits and Systems, vol. 2 (1999)

11. Gill, B.S., Modha, D.S.: SARC: sequential prefetching in adaptive replacement cache. In: USENIX Annual Technical Conference, General Track, pp. 293–308 (2005)
12. Cao, P., et al.: A study of integrated prefetching and caching strategies. ACM SIGMETRICS Perform. Eval. Rev. **23**(1), 188–197 (1995)
13. Curewitz, K.M., et al.: Practical prefetching via data compression. ACM SIGMOD Rec. **22**, 257–266 (1993)
14. Griffioen, J., Appleton, R.: Performance measurements of automatic prefetching. In: Parallel and Distributed Computing Systems, pp. 165–170 (1995)
15. Madhyastha, T.M.: Automatic Classification of Input/Output Access Patterns. Ph.D. thesis, University of Illinois at Urbana-Champaign (1997)
16. Madhyastha, T.M., Reed, D.A.: Input/output access pattern classification using hidden Markov models. In: Proceedings of the Fifth Workshop on I/O in Parallel and Distributed Systems, pp. 57–67. ACM (1997)
17. Yang, S., et al.: Tombolo: performance enhancements for cloud storage gateways. In: Proceedings of the 32nd International Conference on Massive Storage Systems and Technology (MSST 2016) (2016)
18. Li, Z., et al.: C-miner: Mining block correlations in storage systems. In: FAST, vol. 4, pp. 173–186 (2004)
19. Kuenning, G.H., Popek, G.J.: Automated hoarding for mobile computers, vol. 31. ACM (1997)
20. Grimsrud, K.S., et al.: Multiple prefetch adaptive disk caching. IEEE Trans. Knowl. Data Eng. **5**(1), 88–103 (1993)
21. Joseph, D., Grunwald, D.: Prefetching using Markov predictors. In: Proceedings of the 24th Annual International Symposium on Computer Architecture, ISCA 1997, pp. 252–263 (1997)
22. Palmer, M., Zdonik, S.B.: Fido: a cache that learns to fetch. Brown University, Department of Computer Science (1991)
23. Kroeger, T.M., Long, D.D.: Design and implementation of a predictive file prefetching algorithm. In: USENIX Annual Technical Conference, General Track
24. He, J., et al.: Knowac: I/O prefetch via accumulated knowledge. In: 2012 IEEE International Conference on Cluster Computing (CLUSTER), pp. 429–437. IEEE (2012)
25. Vitter, J.S., Krishnan, P.: Optimal prefetching via data compression. J. ACM **43**(5), 771–793 (1996)
26. Lei, H., Duchamp, D.: An analytical approach to file prefetching. In: USENIX Annual Technical Conference, pp. 275–288 (1997)
27. Lin, L., et al.: AMP: an affinity-based metadata prefetching scheme in large-scale distributed storage systems. In: 8th IEEE International Symposium on Cluster Computing and the Grid, CCGRID 2008, pp. 459–466. IEEE (2008)
28. Gu, P., et al.: Nexus: a novel weighted-graph-based prefetching algorithm for metadata servers in petabyte-scale storage systems. In: 6th IEEE International Symposium on Cluster Computing and the Grid, CCGRID 2006, vol. 1, pp. 409–416. IEEE (2006)
29. Cortes, T., Labarta, J.: Linear aggressive prefetching: a way to increase the performance of cooperative caches. In: Proceedings of the 13th International Parallel Processing Symposium and 10th Symposium on Parallel and Distributed Processing, IPPS/SPDP, pp. 46–54. IEEE (1999)
30. Dahlgren, F., et al.: Fixed and adaptive sequential prefetching in shared memory multiprocessors. In: International Conference on Parallel Processing, ICPP 1993, vol. 1, pp. 56–63. IEEE (1993)

31. He, J., et al.: I/O acceleration with pattern detection. In: Proceedings of the 22nd International Symposium on High-Performance Parallel and Distributed Computing, pp. 25–36. ACM (2013)
32. Miller, J.A., Ramaswamy, L., Kochut, K.J., Fard, A.: Directions for big data graph analytics research. Int. J. Big Data 2(1) (2015)
33. Griffioen, J., Appleton, R.: Reducing file system latency using a predictive approach. In: USENIX Summer, pp. 197–207 (1994)
34. Oly, J., Reed, D.A.: Markov model prediction of I/O requests for scientific applications. In: Proceedings of the 16th International Conference on Supercomputing, pp. 147–155. ACM (2002)

Boundless Application and Resource Based on Container Technology

Zhenguang Yu$^{(\boxtimes)}$, Jingyu Wang, Qi Qi, Jianxin Liao, and Jie Xu

State Key Laboratory of Networking and Switching Technology,
Beijing University of Posts and Telecommunications,
Beijing 100876, People's Republic of China
{yuzhenguang,wangjingyu,qiqi,liaojianxin,
xujie}@ebupt.com

Abstract. Limitations like network latency and expensive cost are pushing cloud computing to the edge. Edge computing, also known as fog computing is an extension of cloud computing, providing features to solve problems of cloud computing. However, edge computing is unstable and not enough reliable at present. Orchestration may occur occasionally in order to meet the need of the users. This paper provides an architecture named Boundless Resource Orchestrator (BRO) combing cloud computing and edge computing based on containers. Containers provide more lightweight virtualization compared to VMs. The proposed architecture leverages container technology to accelerate and optimize the orchestration process taking container as the basic component of orchestrating and minimum resource unit for service distribution. A master-slave paradigm is implemented in the architecture to provide region autonomy abilities rather than the centralized architecture. Considering the ever-changing circumstance of edge cloud, an orchestration strategy named Best Performance at Least Cost (BPLC) is proposed to maximize the performance of computing at minimum cost dynamically and automatically considering real-time conditions of the cloud. Experiments are carried out on measuring couples of infrastructures and orchestration strategies that prove the BRO and BPLC as prior choices dealing with massive jobs in edge computing.

Keywords: Containers · Edge computing · Cloud computing · Orchestration

1 Introduction

Resources are spread across datacenters, enterprise clusters and Internet of Things (IoT) devices. Cloud computing virtualize datacenters and provide massive computing resource but at a relatively high cost. Edge computing reorganized and made sufficient use of computing resource in enterprise clusters, personal laptop and IoT devices among the edge, avoiding waste of edge resource and cut costs on using computing resource. Having their own pros and cons, computation offloading is an acceptable solution to reach high performance and utilize of resource statically. However, conditions such as computation overload, internet bandwidth and connection latency may change over time. Applications may have better performance running on the edge now and even better in the cloud second later. Thus, real-time re-scheduling between cloud and edge or redirecting among the edge is needed.

Migration should retain integrity and consistency of the application. Considering the cost of migration and a variety of problems such as dependency loss and mutable situations we may encounter during migrating, a lightweight virtualization solution other than VM is needed [14]. Containerization is currently discussed as a frequently used lightweight virtualization solution [16, 17]. Containers provide more interoperable, standardized and lightweight application packing in the cloud which reduces the overhead of application migration, for example, less time-consuming [13]. Standardized with container technology, application and resource are simpler to manage across the cloud. Containerized application could be distributed with restrictions on resource usage set in advance to scheduled compute node. Furthermore, containers are enough reliable and private to make the isolation of various applications easy [15]. Most orchestration strategy on containers in the edge cloud [3] orchestrates the applications with a scheduler in the data center ignoring different demands of various edge clouds. Strategies may be difficult to formulate due to the ever-changing circumstance of different edge clouds.

Regarding for the challenge of minimizing computing overhead and effectively utilize resource on the edge, we come up with a new research on improving the performance of dynamic re-scheduling between cloud and edge and among edge. Our proposal is to build a modular system architecture, named Boundless Application an Resource Orchestrator (BRO), aims at provisioning application to suitable edge node or to the cloud automatically and dynamically to reach either best performance or best utilization of resource based on container technology. The orchestration depends on multiple parameters such as computation overload, internet bandwidth and the cost of resources. The presented architecture considers single container as the minimum unit of scheduling and a basic resource unit for service distribution. Containerized application is available in a public registry maintained in the core cloud. Distribution and deployment could be done in one click and are transparent to the end users. We implement a master-slave paradigm instead of traditional centralized scheduling setting associate schedulers in each edge cloud running different strategies according to the circumstance of specified edge cloud. Schedulers will make an overall consideration combining the parameters set in advance and real-time conditions on switching containerized application between cloud and edge or across the edge to ensure the performance of the containerized application meet the need of users in minimum cost. Edge devices are able to share idle resources by acting as a pseudo node of the architecture.

Ultimately, the paper put forward an attempt to make resource and application boundless, referring that all resource across the cloud and the edge is managed and could be efficiently used. Applications are somewhere to gain best performance with least cost automatically and dynamically under the proposed architecture. The remainder of this paper is organized as follows. Section 2 lists the related works. Section 3 shows the modular system architecture. Section 4 reveals the details on the implementation of the dedicated system architecture and algorithms included. In Sect. 5, we evaluate the impact of using our architecture on top of different use cases with various aspects taken into consideration. Section 6 concludes the paper and looks into the future work.

2   Related Works

2.1   Edge Computing

Edge Computing is an emerging computational architecture that shares an idea on moving the computation closer to the edge devices in order to avoid limitations such as bandwidth, latency and high cost in traditional cloud computing. Edge computing act as an extension of traditional cloud computing, coming up with the multi-cloud paradigm in line with the trend of decentralization and IoT. In constant to traditional cloud computing, edge computing orchestrates resource and computation on the edge as well as provide all services in a distributed way. Research on edge computing [8, 11, 12] has proved that edge computing meets the demand for computing architecture through now to the future and edge computing is currently widely accepted as an optional infrastructure of IoT [10]. In [9], a strategy for automatic task sharing and switching between cloud and edge computing has been put forward and a smart IoT gateway is designed based on machine learning and cognitive analytics to make an orchestration for applications between the cloud and the edge. However, orchestration on applications in edge computing may be difficult due to the diversity of edge devices and mutable circumstance.

2.2   Container in Edge Computing

Container technology is a widely accepted lightweight virtualization solution which provides isolation, standardization and flexibility with least overhead in cloud computing. Researches shows that the characteristic and advantages of container technology perfectly match the requirements of the edge computing technology on virtualization. In [5], a performance evaluation is done on container technology as the virtualization method in IoT edge architecture. The research shows that container-virtualization technology produces negligible impact in terms of performance when compared to native executions but can enhance IoT security. In [1, 7], other technical evaluation and experiment on specified fundamental edge computing using case is made and claim Docker container as a viable candidate for edge computing architecture while still having rooms for improvement. In general, container technology, providing more security, isolation and higher performance, is the optimal choice rather than VM in edge computing. Researches on the orchestration of containers in edge computing [2–4, 6] are in progress as well. Common orchestration strategy is making scheduling decisions by a scheduler in the core cloud and delivers containers to separate edge nodes considering dynamic circumstance, appearing to be cumbersome and inefficient in contrast to native orchestration on edge computing.

3   Architecture Design

Cloud computing is moving from centralized to the decentralized pattern to avoid network bottleneck and efficiently utilize edge computing resource. Boundless application and resource system is an architecture attempting high performance though scheduling applications between the cloud and the edge or among the edge based on container technology (Fig. 1).

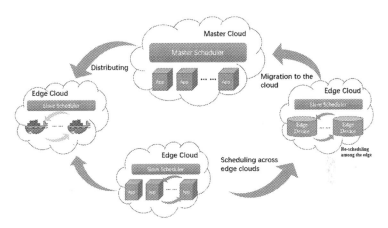

Fig. 1. Architecture of BRO

BRO has the following features:

- Based on container: considering container as the basic unit of application and resource management and scheduling.
- High adaptability: supports various edge devices from enterprise server to personal laptop. Any edge devices that support container can play a role in the architecture.
- High-performance dynamic scheduling strategy: taking real-time condition into consideration, applies suitable mechanism such as BPLC mechanism and tagging mechanism corresponding to different scenarios to achieve the best performance at minimum cost dynamically.
- Sufficient utilize of edge resource through sharing rule: leveraging container technology, it is able to share idle resources of your server or even your laptop.
- Fault tolerant: improve the stability and reliability of the architecture through a complete set of recovery mechanism.

3.1   Containers

Compare to cloud computing, edge computing could be relatively unstable and unreliable. Due to the complex network and heterogeneous structure of edge cloud, the environment of edge computing may change time to time. Widely discussed as an outstanding lightweight virtualization solution, container technology provide isolation for applications among changeable environment with much lower overhead than VMs. While the performance of the application is affected by the real-time condition, re-scheduling is common in edge computing to achieve higher performance. Containerizing application makes scheduling simple. Container technology could provide standardize, isolation, less overhead and high fault tolerant for edge computing, leaving dependency problems behind. Managing distributed containerized application could be implemented as same as managing container clusters in the cloud. Thus, containers are even suitable for the circumstance of edge computing and cloud computing.

3.2 Pseudo Node

BRO aims at making application and resource boundless implying making remote resource reachable and local resource sharable. The most straightforward method is attaching your devices to the cloud, afterward, cloud computing resource is next to your hand. However, joining the cloud is too cumbersome for edge devices and may lead to many problems. As the name suggests, pseudo node initializes the edge device as an incomplete or fake minion with strong restrictions. If the edge device has been initialized to a pseudo node, we can participate in BRO, gain cloud computing resource and share local resources among the cloud portable and safe.

3.3 Regional Autonomy

BRO applies the concept of regional autonomy in edge computing in order to deal with the ever-changing circumstance of the edge cloud. According to the concept of regional autonomy, the architecture divides the edge into different portions according to various properties and characteristic such as logical or physical location, computation overhead and stability. Scheduling will be first done within current portion of edge cloud and then across the edge if lack of resource. Regional autonomy could improve the performance of scheduling efficiency and accuracy as well as be easy to adapt to diverse infrastructures.

4 Implementation

See Fig. 2.

4.1 Application and Resource Unit Management

BRO takes container as the basic unit of application and resource management. All application running under this architecture should be containerized. Thus, we can manage application in a similar way with containers.

Application migration could be simply implemented by transferring container images, which is so small and the state of the application will be stored in the container image. Leveraging orientated scheduling of container cluster is another solution for containerized application migration. The application manager records the behaviors of the containerized application and generates a dockerfile, responsible for lifecycle

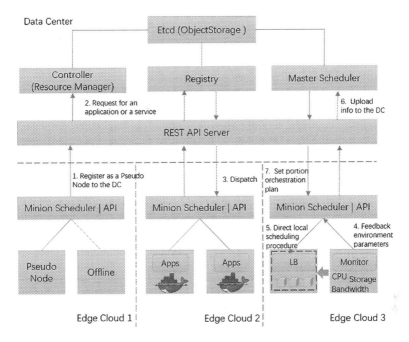

Fig. 2. Lifecycle of edge computing under BRO

management of the containerized application. Application rollback could be implemented by going through the dockerfile.

Container preconfigured a threshold of resource usage referring the maximum resource the application could occupy using cgroup and namespace [20]. Thus, a container can be a unit to measure resource. A special container with the same configuration can be distributed to the objective node to test the resource before the containerized application is scheduled.

4.2   Monitor Container

Monitor container is a special container created during initializing pseudo node. Monitor container consists of various data collectors and several tools for testing, pressure test and heartbeat detection, for example. A pseudo node is considered unavailable when the monitor container is down.

The monitor container supervises the pseudo node and containerized application running upon and is responsible for collecting real-time condition data such as CPU usage, memory usage and I/O usage. Monitor container uploads real-time condition data to the scheduler as a critical counter for the producing of scheduling strategy (Tables 1 and 2).

Monitor container will provide the performance of containerized applications scheduled on current pseudo node to the learning module of the scheduler to optimize the algorithm. If low performance or congestion is detected, the monitor container will

Table 1. Sets used in this article

Sets	Domain
X	Set of nodes
C	Set of nodes in the data center
E	Set of nodes in the edge cloud
S	Set of nodes in the current edge cloud
A	Set of applications
J	Set of jobs
I	Set of types of resources

Table 2. Common condition data referenced by the scheduler.

Notations	Meaning
δ_{uv}	Available bandwidth of route uv, where $u, v \in X$
T_x^1	Total available computational capacity of node x. $x \in X$
T_x^2	Total available memory of node x. $x \in X$
T_x^3	Total available storage of node x. $x \in X$
S_x	Available rate of node x. $x \in X$
l_{uv}	Latency between node u and node v, where $u, v \in X$
O_a	Average data transmission overhead scheduling containerized application a

inform the scheduler to reschedule the containerized applications in time and send feedback for better performance.

Monitor container plays an important role in the tag system. It tries to quantify data collected and add various tags to the pseudo node such as "stable" for pseudo nodes with sustained connectivity and "massive" for pseudo nodes with massive computing resources. Besides the default data collector, self-defined collectors are available for special cases. Before scheduling, a monitor container with a self-defined collector will be delivered to suitable nodes for addition dedicate condition data. Self-defined tags could be added by self-defined collectors for further sharing and scheduling.

4.3 Master-Slave Paradigm

BRO implements regional autonomy through the master-slave paradigm. In contrast to the traditional centralized paradigm, master-slave paradigm divides the edge into parts according to the characteristic and property of the certain range of edge. Each edge cloud owns a dedicate associate scheduler apart from the master scheduler in the data center. The associate scheduler has a set of independent scheduling mechanisms depending on the property and characteristic of the edge cloud. Containerized application could gain best performance scheduling among the edge cloud under the dedicate scheduling mechanism. The associate scheduler runs under the monitor of the master scheduler in the data center. While current edge cloud cannot meet the requirement of the job, the associate scheduler will call for the master scheduler to make an orchestration across different edge clouds or upload to the data center. The master scheduler is also reasonable of instructing associate scheduler and adjusting edge scheduling mechanism analyzing feedback uploaded to the data center. Through master-slave paradigm, BRO implemented regional autonomy and retains the benefits of decentralization. Equation (1) shows default clustering mechanism to divide the edge. L^i and L^1 respectively represent self-defined thresholds for corresponding dimensions.

$$\left\{ e | T_e^i < L^i, \ l_{ue} < L^1, \ u \in S, \ i = 1, 2, 3 \right\} \tag{1}$$

4.4 Scheduling Strategy

Conditions of the cloud may change in time. An application may have fine performance running on the edge for some time and have even better performance running in the cloud for some other time. Thus, scheduling is required to achieve the best performance at all time. Scheduling under BRO consists of scheduling between the cloud and the edge and among the edge, while cloud resource is commonly known as stable, massive but expensive and edge resource usually unstable, unreliable but low-cost.

The scheduler is responsible for generating scheduling strategies and initiating a scheduling procedure through commanding the built-in scheduler of the container cluster to schedule the target application. Scheduling strategy under BRO is usually divided into two categories: static strategy and dynamic strategy. As the platform is initialized statically and relatively stable, applications are initially scheduled under the static strategy. Once real-time conditions such as computing overhead, internet bandwidth or connectivity changes, the dynamic strategy should be used.

A traditional solution is categorizing the containerized applications manually into few types such as high traffic or heavy computation, which brings lack of accuracy. BRO guides the scheduling process according to the Best Performance at Least Cost (BPLC) algorithm with the assistance of a tagging mechanism. BPLC aims at gaining best performance at least cost through effective scheduling of containerized applications. The performance could be measured through the average job finishing time. Average job finishing time is made up of the average job waiting time implying scheduling overhead and average job execution time that depends on resource conditions. Scheduling overhead depends on latency l_{uv} and data transmission overhead O_a. We express average job execution time using resource conditions of the edge. Equation (2) shows the performance of the static scheduling strategy and Eq. (3) shows the performance of the dynamic scheduling strategy. α, β and γ are tuning parameters for the weight of the separate parts.

$$\alpha \sum_{i=1,2,3} \gamma_i \sum_{e \in S} T_e^i - \beta \left(\sum_{e \in S} \min_{c \in C} l_{ce} + \sum_{a \in A} O_a \right) \tag{2}$$

$$\alpha \sum_{i=1,2,3} \gamma_i \sum_{e \in S} T_e^i - \beta \left(\sum_{e_1 \in S} \min_{e_2 \in S} l_{e_1 e_2} + \sum_{a \in A} O_a \right) \tag{3}$$

Except gaining best performance, BPLC attempts to reduce the cost of running applications in the edge cloud. We assume the cost on the device in the edge mainly depend on the resource it provides. Cost of running applications is measured as Eq. (4). S_a represents edge nodes occupied running application a and R_a^i respectively represent resources required by application a.

$$\sum_i \varepsilon_i \sum_{e \in S_a} T_e^i \tag{4}$$

Considering both performance and the cost, object function of BPLC is shown as Eq. (5). Equation (6)–(7) reveal part of the constraints such as bandwidth conservation and computational resource conservation. a_{uv} represents application scheduling through node u and node v.

$$\max \alpha \sum_{e \in S_a} \gamma_i \sum_{i=1,2,3} \sum_{e \in S_a} T_e^i - \beta \left(\sum_{e_1 \in S_a} \min_{e_2 \in S, e_2 \notin S_a} l_{ce} + \sum_{a \in A} O_a \right) - \theta \sum_i \varepsilon_i \sum_{e \in S_a} T_e^i \tag{5}$$

$$\sum_{a_{e_1 e_2} \in A,} O_{a_{e_1 e_2}} \le \delta_{e_1 e_2} \; \forall e_1, e_2 \in S_a \tag{6}$$

$$\sum_{e \in S_a} T_e^i > R_a^i \forall i \in I \tag{7}$$

Tagging mechanism act as a supplement to the BPLC algorithm. According to the tagging mechanism, pseudo nodes on the edge is tagged during initialization by the monitor container according to the instant condition of the devices such as computing resource available, internet bandwidth and connection persistency and stability. Application managers add tags to the containerized application according to the demand of the application, massive or long living, for example. Though comparing the tags, combing the overhead of migration and suitability of the pseudo node, it is easy to determine a target node for scheduling.

However, common tags cannot cover the massive properties on demand. We come up with customized tags added by monitor containers with self-defined data collectors enriching the properties covered. With increasing amount of tags, fuzzy matching of tags is effective but not efficient enough. The problem is that it is hard to match tags on application to various customized tags. We put forward a new tagging mechanism based on machine learning. Before scheduling, we run a simulation container that acts as the same as the target containerized application on a sample node with a comprehensive monitor container. The dedicate monitor container is trained with a machine learning algorithm, classifying all customize tags and extract features. After a period, the dedicate monitor container will analyze the behavior of the specified testing container and add a group of customized tags with the corresponding features. The whole tagging procedure is done automatically and will be more accurate with time. Feedback such as error report and operational situation sent by monitor containers across the edge can further improve the performance of the new tagging mechanism. Nevertheless, additional overhead is required for the first time the containerized application is scheduled.

5 Experiment and Use Case

We present two case study respectively to examine master-slave paradigm and regional autonomy as an impressive orchestration pattern for edge computing architecture based on containers and estimate the strategy mentioned in scheduling containerized applications.

5.1 Examining Effects of Master-Slave Paradigm

We setup a lab environment as showed at Fig. 3 with a datacenter and four groups of edge devices ranges from dedicate servers to personal laptop. We use *Docker* [18] as an implement of container technology and deploy a container cluster with *Kubernetes* in the datacenter as the basic core cloud. *Kubernetes* [19] is a production grade container orchestration tool and is the best solution to act as the native container cluster manager in our architecture. Node manager, application manager and scheduler in our architecture will implement upon the native container cluster manager we choose, *Kubernetes* during this experiment, for example.

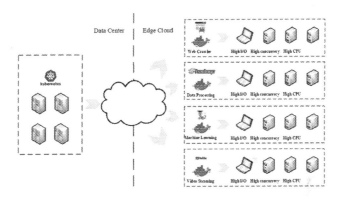

Fig. 3. Topology of lab environment

Edge devices are initialized to pseudo nodes, as a fake minion of the container cluster. Each edge devices will have different properties: group a has least computing overload, group b has low network latency, group c has maximum internet bandwidth and group d is balanced on all properties. All edge devices are reachable by another and accessible from the container cluster.

In this experiment, we created a group of containers running machine learning and another group of containers running web crawlers program through the *dockerfile* and randomly deploy them among the edge devices. In reality, containerized applications should be pushed to the public registry in the cloud and deployed from the datacenter to the edge cluster. We deploy them directly among the edge devices for convenience to observe the scheduling procedure.

Four set of experiments is taken following the same procedure mentioned before under various infrastructure. We take VM, native environment and centralized paradigm as parallel experiments to the master-slave paradigm. We respectively record job average waiting time and job average execution time running different amount of jobs. Job average waiting time implies the time cost of scheduling and job average execution time indicates the performance of the architecture. We use the number of jobs to simulate the scale of the computation and observe the performance of four infrastructure under different circumstance.

The outcome of the experiment proves container technology as an effective solution providing isolation, reducing scheduling overhead and fastening the scheduling procedure. Containerized application could be a choice under edge computing scenario. According to the record in Figs. 4 and 5, we can temporarily draw some conclusions:

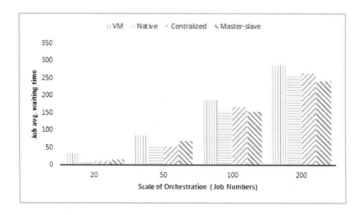

Fig. 4. Job average waiting time in different scale of orchestration

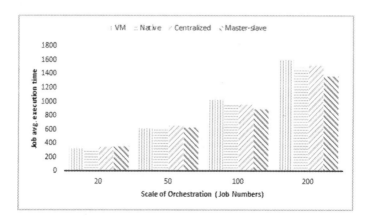

Fig. 5. Job average execution time in different scale of orchestration

- Container technology cuts the overhead of scheduling and is a better choice compared traditional VMs. However, container technology makes negligible improvement in terms of performance compared to native executions.

- Master-slave paradigm acts similar to the centralized paradigm in small scale but gains better performance with the increase in the number of jobs.
- Master-slave paradigm accelerates scheduling and owns high accuracy comparing to centralized paradigm dealing with massive jobs. Regional autonomy contributes to this feature while dealing each edge cloud with more suitable strategy.

5.2   Estimating BPLC Associated with Tagging Mechanism

In order to estimate the effectiveness of tag mechanism under the circumstance mentioned in the paper, we present a case study to compare the tag mechanism with the native container scheduling method and IoT gateway [9] without containers.

We setup a lab environment with a datacenter and four groups of edge devices. The datacenter is initialized as same as the former experiment and the edge devices are given random combinations of properties such as high internet bandwidth with high computing overload or low computing overload with less network latency.

After initializing the lab environment, we create a group of containers running different types of applications ranging from high traffic to high computing overload. We deploy them from the datacenter to get a clear view of the scheduling procedure between cloud and edge and among edge.

We will repeat the experiment procedure three times respectively with native container orchestration mechanism, BPLC mechanism and IoT gateway and record a set of data. The statistic of the result is revealed in Figs. 6 and 7.

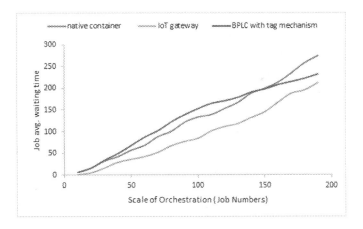

Fig. 6. Job average waiting time under different orchestration strategy

According to the result recorded, Job avg. waiting time reveals the total time spent scheduling the jobs to suitable nodes. The BPLC mechanism takes a little more time in small scale but shows better performance than native container orchestration mechanism along with the growth of jobs. IoT gateway owns least waiting time cause of none overhead. Job avg. execution time shows the performance of the jobs. Statistic reveals that BPLC mechanism performs much better than the others especially with massive

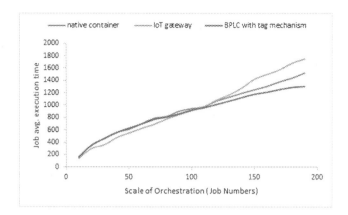

Fig. 7. Job average execution time under different orchestration strategy

jobs, claiming the accuracy of the orchestration and high resource utilization of edge resource. The outcome of the experiment proves that the BPLC mechanism proposed in the paper is effective in scheduling containerized application among the edge cloud.

5.3   Use Case

BRO owns strong adaptability and could be widely adopted by companies, public organizations and even personal laptops. Use cases of BRO vary from applying as an enhanced implementation of IoT scenarios such as Smart Cities, E-health and smart homes to acting as an invisible frame making resource gaining and application running automatic and convenient for the public.

A common use case is acting as an invisible frame contributing to accelerating the automatic process of application orchestrating and resource utilize optimization. For example, training a model for a deep learning job could be finished within one-step setting parameters with a template. The specified job will be initialized, containerized and orchestrated to suitable nodes for best performance without the intervention of operators. Other use cases include but not limited to idle resource liquidation, traffic shaving and fast deployment.

6   Conclusion and Future Work

This paper has put forward an architecture based on container technology aims at combing cloud computing and edge computing. Appling container technology in edge computing effectively increases stability and performance through optimizing the orchestration procedure, lower the cost of scheduling. BRO attempts to deliver applications to suitable edge node or to the cloud automatically and dynamically to reach either best performance or best utilize of resource based on container technology. Rather than centralized dispatching from the data center, the master-slave paradigm is much more elastic, reliable and effective while regional autonomy can be better adapted to the ever-changing environment of edge computing. Furthermore, orchestration strategy BPLC with tagging mechanism is designed for edge computing under the container-based architecture and improves the performance of cloud computing and edge computing.

Currently, there are still limits accessing resources in the cloud or among the edge due to plenty of problems such as security problems. The emergence of BRO and BPLC solves these problems slightly but not completely. Future work place emphasis on improving the performance of container in edge computing and optimizing dedicate orchestration strategy under various circumstances. Hopefully, resource and application will be standardized and reachable anywhere in the visible future.

Acknowledgment. This work was jointly supported by: (1) National Natural Science Foundation of China (No. 61771068, 61671079, 61471063, 61372120, 61421061); (2) Beijing Municipal Natural Science Foundation (No.4182041, 4152039); (3) the National Basic Research Program of China (No. 2013CB329102).

References

1. Ismail, B., Mostajeran, E., Bazli Ab Karim, M., Ming Tat, W., Setapa, S., Luke, J.-Y., Ong, H.: Evaluation of docker as edge computing platform (2015)
2. Pahl, C., Lee, B.: Containers and clusters for edge cloud architectures – a technology review (2015). https://doi.org/10.1109/ficloud.2015.35
3. Dupont, C., Giaffreda, R., Capra, L.: Edge computing in IoT context: horizontal and vertical Linux container migration, pp. 1–4 (2017)
4. Park, J.-W., Hahm, J., Container-based cluster management platform for distributed computing. In: Proceedings of the International Conference on Parallel and Distributed Processing Techniques and Applications, pp. 34–40 (2015)
5. Morabito, R.: Virtualization on internet of things edge devices with container technologies: a performance evaluation (2017)
6. Morabito, R., Beijar, N.: Enabling data processing at the network edge through lightweight virtualization technologies (2016)
7. Xavier, M.G., Neves, M.V., Rossi, F.D., Ferreto, T.C., Lange, T., De Rose, C.A.F.: Performance evaluation of container-based virtualization for high performance computing environments. In: Proceedings of the 2013 21st Euromicro International Conference on Parallel, Distributed, and Network-Based Processing, PDP 2013, pp. 233–240. IEEE Computer Society, Washington, DC (2013)
8. Jalali, F., Hinton, K., Ayre, R., Alpcan, T., Tucker, R.S.: Fog computing may help to save energy in cloud computing. IEEE J. Sel. Areas Commun. (2016)
9. Jalali, F., Smith, O.J, Lynar, T., Suits, F.: Cognitive IoT gateways: automatic task sharing and switching between cloud and edge/fog computing (2017)
10. Cozzolino, V., Ding, A.Y., Ott, J., Kutscher, D.: Enabling fine-grained edge offloading for IoT (2017)
11. Kosta, S., Aucinas, A., Hui, P., Mortier, R., Zhang, X.: ThinkAir: dynamic resource allocation and parallel execution in the cloud for mobile code offloading. In: 2012 Proceedings IEEE INFOCOM, pp. 945–953 (2012)
12. Kniess, J.: Reducing web application latency with fog computing (2016)

13. Zheng, C., Thain, D.: Integrating containers into workflows: a case study using makeflow, work queue, and docker. In: Proceedings of the 8th International Workshop on Virtualization Technologies in Distributed Computing, VTDC 2015, pp. 31–38. ACM, New York (2015)
14. Felter, W., Ferreira, A., Rajamony, R., Rubio, J.: An updated performance comparison of virtual machines and Linux containers. In: Performance Analysis of Systems and Software (ISPASS), pp. 171–172 (2015)
15. Gerlach, W., Tang, W., Keegan, K., Harrison, T., Wilke, A., Bischof, J., D'Souza, M., Devoid, S., Murphy-Olson, D., Desai, N., Meyer, F.: Skyport: container-based execution environment management for multi-cloud scientific workflows. In: Proceedings of the 5th International Workshop on Data-Intensive Computing in the Clouds, DataCloud 2014, pp. 25–32. IEEE Press, Piscataway (2014)
16. Bernstein, D.: Containers and cloud: From LXC to docker to kubernetes. IEEE Cloud Comput. 1(3), 81–84 (2014)
17. Alfonso, C., Calatrava, A., Moltó, G.: Container-based virtual elastic clusters. J. Syst. Softw. 127, 1–11 (2017)
18. Docker. https://www.docker.com/. Accessed 22 Mar 2018
19. Kubernetes. http://kubernetes.io/. Accessed 23 Mar 2018
20. Linux containers, https://linuxcontainers.org/. Accessed 19 Feb 2018

A Reconfigurable Streaming Processor for Real-Time Low-Power Execution of Convolutional Neural Networks at the Edge

Justin Sanchez[✉], Nasim Soltani, Pratik Kulkarni,
Ramachandra Vikas Chamarthi, and Hamed Tabkhi

University of North Carolina at Charlotte, Charlotte, NC, USA
jsanch19@uncc.edu

Abstract. With the recent advances in machine learning and the deep learning paradigm, there is a huge demand to push the data analytics and cognitive inference to the edge of the network near the data producers and sensors. Edge analytics are essential for real-time video analytics and situational awareness; which is required for the wide range of cyber-physical applications such as smart transportation, smart cities, and smart health. To this end, novel architectures and platforms are required to enable real-time low-power deep learning execution at the edge.

This paper introduces a novel reconfigurable architecture for real-time execution of deep learning and in particular convolutional Neural Networks (CNNs) at the edge of the network, close to the video camera. The proposed architecture offers a set of coarse-grain function blocks required for realizing CNN algorithms. The macro-pipelined datapath is created by chaining the function blocks with respect to the topology of the target network. The function blocks operate over the streaming pixels (directly fed from the camera interface) in a producer/consumer fashion. At the same time, function blocks offer enough flexibility to adjust the processing with respect to area, power, and performance requirements. This paper primarily focuses on the two first layers of CNNs as the two most compute-intensive layers of CNN network. Our implementation on Xilinx Zynq FPGAs, for the first two layers of the SqueezNet Network, shows 315 mW power consumption when designed at 30 fps, with only a 0.24 ms one-time-latency. In contrast, the Nvidia Tegra TX2 GPU is limited to perform at 32.2 fps due to the 31.4 ms delay, with a much higher power consumption (7.5 W).

1 Introduction

Deep learning paradigm has emerged as a promising scalable machine learning solution for extensive data analytics and inference [1–4]. Many applications from smart transportation, and smart and connected communities, inherently require

© Springer International Publishing AG, part of Springer Nature 2018
S. Liu et al. (Eds.): EDGE 2018, LNCS 10973, pp. 49–64, 2018.
https://doi.org/10.1007/978-3-319-94340-4_4

real-time or near real-time scalable deep-learning inference. One major example is real-time video analytic for object localization, detection, and classification. With the tight latency requirements, long communication latency, and scarcity of communication bandwidth, the cloud comping paradigm is not able to offer a scalable sustainable solution for real-time deep learning inference. Therefore, novel architecture and design paradigms are required to push deep learning from the cloud to the edge of the network near to the data producers (e.g. video cameras).

While GPUs are widely used for training, they are not an efficient platform for real-time deep learning inference at the edge. GPUs are inherently throughput-oriented machines which makes them less suitable for the edge. GPUs require the large batch size of data (multiple video frames) to achieve high performance and power efficiency. Furthermore, GPUs have lack of deterministic execution patterns; [5,6]. To overcome the limitations of GPUs, we have seen many new custom hardware approaches for accelerating deep learning inference. Few industrial examples are Google TPU [7], and Microsoft Brainwave [8]. While these platforms offered much higher performance and power efficiency compared to GPUs they still rely on throughput-oriented processing principles, which is more suitable for cloud computing, than the real-time inference at the edge. There is a need for novel custom platforms that offers latency-aware scalable acceleration for real-time deep-learning analytics over streaming data at the edge.

In this paper, we propose a novel reconfigurable architecture template for real-time low-power execution of Convolutional Neural Networks (CNNs) in the edge devices next to the camera. In principle, our proposed architecture is a coarse-grain dataflow machine, which performs CNN computation over streaming pixels. It consists of basic functional blocks required for CNN processing. The blocks are configurable with respect to data window size (size of convolution) and stride, and other network hyperparameters. The macro data-path is constructed by proper chaining of the function blocks with respect to targeted network topology. Function blocks are fused together and work concurrently to realize the convolutional operations without the need to store the streaming pixels in the memory hierarchy. Furthermore, the architecture provides enough configurability to adjust itself to rapidly growing and continuously evolving CNN topologies. As a result, the proposed architecture offers a reconfigurable template (rather than a single solution) that is able to generate efficient architecture instances. This feature gives us the possibility of easily adapting the architecture to any desired network topology. Furthermore our architecture works in a streaming fashion with minimum memory access, with respect to the algorithm's intrinsic parallelism.

The major focus of our architecture is on accelerating the first two layers of CNNs, as they are the most compute-intensive kernels. The first two layers will run on the edge device, next to the camera, while other layers will run on the edge server in a proximity to edge devices. Our implementation of Xilinx Zynq FPGAs, for the first two layers of SqueezNet Network [9], shows 315 mW on-chip power consumption with an execution time of 0.24 ms. In contrast, the Nvidia

Tegra TX2 GPU is only able to perform with an execution time of 31.4 ms, with a much higher on-chip power consumption (135 W).

The rest of this paper is organized as follows. Section 2 presents a summary on the existing methods and past literature on architectures for neural networks. Section 3 motivates the proposed architecture. Section 4 explains the details of the proposed architecture. Section 4.4 presents function blocks integration and dimensioning. Section 5 presents our implementation results. Finally, Sect. 6 concludes the paper.

2   Related Work

GPUs' large power consumption conflicts with low power requirements in mobile applications [10–13]. This pushed the designers to use customized hardware accelerators for implementing CNNs at the edge. These custom accelerators could be targeted for ASIC [6] or FPGAs [14]. Most of recent works have focused on converting direct convolution to matrix multiplication. Among them, some have focused on doing the multiplication in a low-latency and low-power manner. Tann et al. [15] propose to map floating-point networks to 8-bit fixed-point networks with integer power-of-two weights and hence to replace multiplication with shift operations to do a low-power and low-latency multiplication.

A number of recent works have addressed this extensive memory requirement and have proposed different methods to reduce this memory access [16]. As some examples, [17] proposes entirely mapping a CNN inside an SRAM, considering weights are shared among many neurons, and eliminate all DRAM accesses for weights. Later authors in [18] proposed a hardware accelerator targeted for FPGAs that exploits sparsity of neuron activation to accelerate computation and reduce external memory accesses. They exploit the flexibility of FPGAs to make their architecture work with different kernel sizes and number of feature maps. Han et al. [19] uses deep compression to fit large networks into on-chip SRAMs and accelerates resulting sparse matrix-vector multiplication by weight sharing. They decrease energy usage by going from DRAMs to SRAMs, exploiting sparsity in multiplication, weight sharing, etc. Jafri et al. [20] presents an architecture targeted for ASIC that exploits the flexibility of compressing and decompressing both input image pixels and kernels to minimize DRAM accesses. They also presents an algorithm (LAMP) that intelligently partitions memory and computational resources of a MOCHA accelerator to map a CNN to it. [21] proposes a convolution engine that achieves energy efficiency by capturing data reuse patterns and enabling a large number of operations per memory access. Authors in [22] propose fusing the processing of multiple CNN layers by modifying the order that input data are brought on chip. They cache intermediate data (data that is transferred between layers) between the evaluations of adjacent CNN layers.

With all these different approaches towards reducing memory access, a lack of an architecture that separates the computation data from memory data and works on the streaming pixels is still sensed. This paper proposes such an architecture that can be further configured for any desirable network topology.

3   Background and Motivation

In this section, we briefly overview data access types in CNN, and the differences between General Matrix Multiplication (GEMM) and direct convolution. We conclude with the motivation to focus on the first two layers of the CNN.

3.1   Data Access Types

Convolutional Neural Networks (CNN) are both memory and compute-intensive applications, often reusing intermediate data and while consistently doing millions of parallel operations. Furthermore, the inherent memory intensive aspects of the algorithm are further exaggerated due to complex multi-dimensional data accesses. In this regard, we consider two major types of data when performing CNN.

(1) **2D Weight:** The first type is 2D weight matrices. These weight matrices each correspond to a single channel and these channels weight matrices group together to construct the entire kernel. Multiple kernels form a layer, and multiple layers create a network topology.
(2) **Frame Pixels:** The streaming pixels which are the input to the CNN processing. Just like the weight matrices these are 2D matrices, with multiple channels. This is the data that flows through the network topology.

3.2   GEMM vs Direct Convolution

Direct convolution is the point-wise Multiply and Accumulation (MAC) operation across the 2D weight Matrices and frame pixels. In direct convolution, similar to the algorithmic level definition, the weight Matrices are used to perform multiple multiply and then accumulation operations directly on the 2D window of input pixels. The direct convolution performs in a sliding window fashion with respect to a stride parameter that varies layer to layer in network topologies. Figure 1 exemplifies direct convolution operation, for a 3 by 3 convolution window over a frame with 5 by 5 pixels.

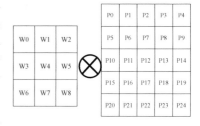

Fig. 1. Direct convolution

Traditionally, GPUs have seen much success in the cloud by using a linear algebra transformation called General Matrix Multiplication (GEMM) to lower the dimensions of convolution to regular matrix multiplication. GEMM transforms all the temporal parallelism into spatial parallelism. This helps GPUs to achieve a high throughput assuming the large data batches are available. However,

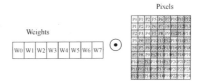

Fig. 2. General Matrix Multiplication (GEMM)

this comes at a significant memory cost. The transformation is done by rearrangement with redundant copies of input image pixels. Our estimation reveals that the rearrangement results in 11X data duplication only for the first layer of any CNN network. This translates to significant power and energy overhead for accessing the redundant pixel data throughout memory hierarchy. Figure 2 exemplifies GEMM operation, for the same example illustrated in Fig. 1. As we observe, redundancy of frame pixels is required to transfer the convolution operation to a large matrix multiplication. For this example, the pixels will be 9 by 9 compared to original frame size which is 5 by 5.

3.3   CNN Execution Bottlenecks

In this paper, we primarily focus on accelerating the first two layers of CNN as the major execution bottlenecks. We specifically target SqueezNet [9], a DCNN design with memory efficiency in mind. To motivate our argument, we have estimated the computation demands across the CNN layers for the example of SqueezNet [9]. Figure 3 shows the computation distribution across the SqueezNet layers. Overall, SqueezNet contains 10 layers. The first and last layers are traditional convolution layers (conv0 and conv9). The intermediate layers are squeeze (s) and expand (e) convolutional layers.

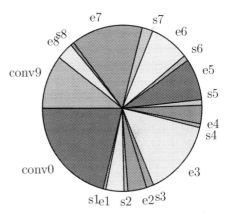

Fig. 3. Computation distribution across the SqueezNet layers

The squeeze layers combine the feature maps to make the network more efficient and expand layers expand the feature map. As we observe, the first layer (conv0) has the highest computation demand with 21% contribution to overall computation demand. The first layer also generates the largest size of feature map across all layers which can lead to significant communication and memory traffic. Figure 4 presents the contribution of layers on feature map. To minimize the memory access and communication demand, it would be beneficial to accelerate the second layer (s1, e1) along with the first layer. In this way, much

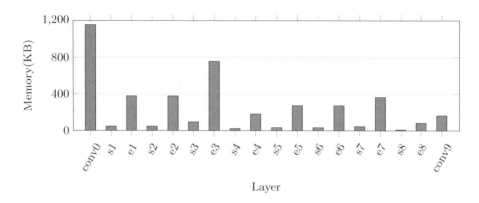

Fig. 4. Feature map distribution

smaller feature maps will be transferred to the edge server for processing of the remaining layers.

4   Architecture Template

This section introduces our proposed architecture template, for real-time execution of CNN inference on the edge. The proposed template targets FPGA devices, as they offer both efficient execution and sufficient reconfigurability to cope with continuously growing CNN topologies [23]. Furthermore, by targeting the FPGAs, we are able to generate a customized datapath per each CNN network as such to best fit the processing requirements. The major premise of our proposed architecture is to remove the gap between the algorithm execution semantic and architecture realization. Therefore, our proposed architecture is primarily a data flow machine working on streaming data based on direct convolution. It consists of three main function blocks for realizing the wide range of CNN inference topological structure. The blocks are Convolutional Processing Element (CPE), Aggregation Processing Element (APE), and Pooling Processing Element (PPE). The blocks will be configured and connected with respect to target network topology, creating a macro-pipeline datapath. Figure 5 presents overall architecture realization from logical domain (algorithm) to physical domain (architecture).

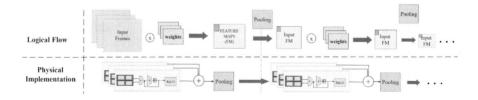

Fig. 5. From algorithm composition to architecture realization.

Our architecture is designed based on the natural dataflow of CNNs. It is able to exploit both spatial parallelism across the convolutions within the same layer, as well as temporal parallelism between the blocks across the layers. The blocks are configurable with respect to network parameters such as size of convolution and stride. This gives us the possibility of easily adapting the architecture to any desired network topology.

In this paper, we focus our architecture realization of the first tow layers of CNNs. While our proposed architecture template is

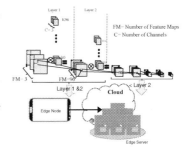

Fig. 6. CNN computation mapping between the edge node and edge server

extensible and can support the entire CNN topology, the primary limitation is available hardware resources on FPGAs of the edge devices. At this moment, we are targeting smaller FPGAs, e.g. Xilinx Zynq [24], with small reconfigurable fabric. However, by accelerating the first two layers on the edge node, we will able to relax the computation demands on the edge server. Figure 6 shows the logical mapping of the network between the edge node and edge devices. The edge node will perform the heavy computation of the first layer. Furthermore, it runs the second layer to significantly shrink the feature map. Then it sends the feature maps to the edge server for the remaining layers to do the processing.

4.1 Covolutional Processing Elements (CPE)

Convolutional Processing Element (CPE) is responsible to perform the primary computation of CNN which is direct convolution over two-dimensional pixel stream. Figure 7 presents the internal architecture of CPE block. It contains two primary blocks: (1) 2D-line Buffer and (2) Multiply and Accumulator (MAC) engines.

2D-Line Buffers. The 2D-line buffer is what enables convolution neural networks to operate in an streaming manner. This is achieved by maintaining the reused pixels for multiple cycles. The pixels that must be reused are determined by the network topology and the receptive field of the layer the 2D line buffer is mapped to. Every layer of a convolutional neural network has a hyperparameter called stride that dictates how the receptive field slides through the feature maps, both horizon-

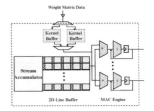

Fig. 7. Convolutional Processing Element

tally and vertically. No matter what the stride is set to, the minimum amount of data that must be stored is determined by the size of the receptive field or filter window. However, when the stride is less than the filter dimension size, extra feature map data must be kept in a buffer.

To deal with the horizontal reuse, only twice the extra pixels must be kept at max, however, vertical stride requires all rows that were used in the filter window to be available. The 2D-line buffer that is used in our approach is able to overcome this by keeping the minimum amount of rows needed. We keep at least one row of the streaming input to preserve the horizontal reuse and we maintain extra rows depending on the filter size in order to preserve the vertical reuse of data. This is done for all streaming feature map data in each layer through the accelerator. The 2D-line buffer is expanded by having an input FIFO which we call stream accumulator to allow the buffer to receive input while operating on the data at the same time.

Multiply and Accumulator (MAC) Engines. The convolution unit is the heart of the architecture. It is composed of a series of independent MAC units that perform parallel multiply and accumulate operations together each cycle. The MAC units are able to execute any kernel size by simply changing the number of cycles it operates on data. These MAC units further enable efficient and flexible convolution by exploiting the multiple forms of parallelism inherent to the convolution operation. The first form of parallelism we exploit is Intra-Kernel parallelism. Intra-Kernel achieved by dividing the convolution of a single kernel to multiple MAC units. By exploiting this parallelism a 7×7 kernel which would normally take 49 cycles can only take 7 cycles, by dedicating 7 MAC units to operate on the pixel and weight data in parallel.

The next form of parallelism, Inter-Kernel parallelism, is achieved by fetching multiple kernels at once and having at least one MAC dedicated to each. The main benefit to this form of parallelism comes when you exploit the full available inter-kernel parallelism. When all kernels are run together the kernel weights can be kept in the buffer thus removing unnecessary memory fetches. The 2D-line buffer allows data0-level parallelism by reusing the same kernel on all the feature map data available on the buffer. This approach leaves less of a memory footprint on the system. Further feature map parallelism is also a possibility by running multiple feature map sections concurrently, however, this would increase the memory footprint left on the main system, so we do leave it to be explored in future work.

4.2 Aggregation Processing Elements (APE)

This layer performs aggregation across multiple output streams representing different channels. Figure 8 presents overall view of our proposed *APE* module. APE is perhaps the simplest functional block in our architecture. It takes the stream of input pixels that have negative and positive values, rectifies the negative values to zero and passes the positive values as they are. Therefore, the output of APE is a non-negative sequence of pixel values.

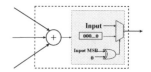

Fig. 8. Aggregation Processing Element (APE)

4.3   Pooling Processing Elements (PPE)

Pooling Processing Elements (PPEs) are in charge of down-sampling the image. Every pooling process has two parameters of stride and window (filter) size. The degree of compression actually depends on the stride. The core idea of pooling with a $n \times n$ window is to replace each window with the maximum among all the elements in that window. Figure 9 shows an example of pooling with the window size of 3×3 and stride of 2.

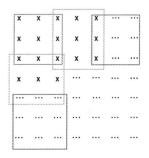

Fig. 9. The sliding window with stride

To avoid the unnecessary memory and buffer requirements to store the entire feature map, the proposed pooling block works on the stream of pixels while supporting variable horizontal and vertical pooling strides. Figure 10 presents the architecture details of our proposed PPE. In the following we will present a detailed description of 3×3 window with a stride of two as an example to illustrate the on-the-fly pooling process. For horizontal stride, the pooling block receives the first pixel and keeps it in a register until the second pixel arrives. When the second pixel arrives, a comparator will compare the two and keeps the result in a register since it is not the end of our window yet. When the third pixel arrives, it is sent to the comparator to determine the maximum of the first three pixels. This maximum is then stored in the FIFO. The third pixel is also kept separately in a register to be compared with pixel 4. (Because in a stride of 2, pixel 3 is shared between the first and second windows.) The same process repeats until all the pixels in the first row are received. By this time, maximum values in each window, for the first row of the image, are stored in the FIFO and the FIFO is full now.

For taking care of vertical stride, when the second row arrives, maximum of the three first pixels is calculated like the first row. However, it is time for the oldest input of the FIFO to pop out. This oldest element would be the maximum of the first window in the first row, which is then compared to our new maximum in the second row and the largest between the two is fed to the FIFO. Similarly,

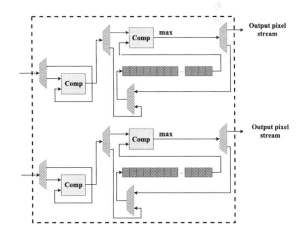

Fig. 10. Pooling Processing Elements (PPE)

when the third row arrives, the process for the second row is repeated and finally, the maximum of all nine pixels in the first window is Fed to the FIFO. Moreover, to take care of the horizontal stride, since the third row is also the horizontal end of our window, as the pixel stream for the third row arrives, we also feed it to another pooling block as the first row of the image. All the process described above is replicated in this second pooling block. The first pooling block is vacated after all the maximums for first row windows are calculated and sent out, and by the time the sixth row arrives, pooling block is ready to receive this row as the first row.

4.4   Function Blocks Integration

The Macro-pipeline consists of single CPEs mapped to one input channel of a layer. The full layer is then constructed by multiple CPEs operating in parallel. The CPEs are then wired together by the APE to aggregate the convolutions and pass data to the next layer. A PPE is optionally generated after the aggregation if the network topology demands it with the data stream then being fed into the multiple CPEs of the next layer.

This MACRO-pipelined datapath is generated layer by layer until the desired network topology is achieved. By changing the number of CPEs we can support multiple layers with multiple channels. Each CPE itself is also able to handle customization to each layer's hyper parameters such as stride, Kernel dimensions and input frame size. The system receives image data directly from the sensor, this allows users to separate the input and memory traffic and minimize the memory footprint. To handle the kernel data we include on-chip memory to double buffer access to the main memory and hide the latency. That becomes an end to end accelerator capable of flexible acceleration over the domain of CNNs.

5   Evaluation

This section presents our evaluation results based on implementation on Xilinx Zynq FPGAs.

5.1   Experimental Setup

The full architecture template was constructed using chisel [25], a high-level hardware construction language. We feed the chisel code multiple parameters of the network topology as well as design parameters on how we should extract the natural parallelism. The code then generates a Macro-pipelined datapath to run the network topology. We have implemented an instance of our architecture template for the first two layers of the SqueezNet [9]. We focused on SqueezNet network because it was designed with computational and memory efficiency. The design was realized with a Xilinx Zynq-7000 FPGA [24], due to its low power footprint and embedded Processor.

Table 1. SqueezNet topology properties for the first two layers.

Layer number	Number of CPEs	Kernel size	Number of MACs	Intra kernel parallelism	Inter kernel parallelism	Frequency (MHz)
0	3	(7 × 7)	49	2	98	71
1	96	(1 × 1)	1	1	1	11

Table 1 presents SqueezNet architecture properties for the first two layers. Overall, the first layer, as the major compute-intensive layer, contains 96 kernels each one performing 7 by 7 convolution which translates to 49 MACs. It also contains three channel representing R, G, and B.

For evaluation, we use three different possible datapaths of our proposed architecture. Figures 11, 12 and 13 shows these three implementations respectively, with respect to our proposed CPE and function block integration presented in Sect. 4. Intra kernel parallelism focuses on spatial parallelism in the MAC operations within each kernel. On the other extreme, inter kernel parallelism solely focuses on the spatial parallelism across MAC operations across all 96 parallel kernels. In between, the hybrid inter/intra kernel parallelism aims to find a balance between inter and intra kernel parallelism.

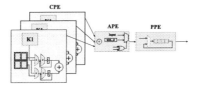

Fig. 11. Intra kernel parallelism

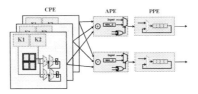

Fig. 12. Inter kernel parallelism

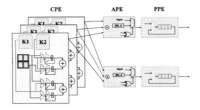

Fig. 13. Hybrid inter/intra kernel parallelism

5.2   Resource Utilization and Power Overhead

This section presents the resource utilization and power overhead for the three proposed configuration.

Figure 14 shows the dynamic power of our proposed architecture when running the first layer for three types of parallelism. The results gathered for real-time processing of 30 frames per second with 227×227 resolution. As the figure illustrates, the intra-kernel parallelism achieves the minimum power consumption by consuming only 135 mW dynamic power consumption. The hybrid parallelism is a close second and inter-kernel parallelism has the highest power consumption. The static power of entire FPGAs is about 180 mW. This leads to the overall power consumption of 315 mW.

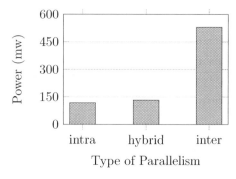

Fig. 14. First layer dynamic power for different types of parallelism

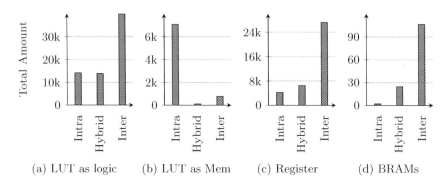

(a) LUT as logic   (b) LUT as Mem   (c) Register   (d) BRAMs

Fig. 15. Absolute FPGAs resource demand for the first layer across design points.

Figure 15 presents the absolute resource consumption for the three design points. Figure 16 also presents relative resource utilization on Xilinx Zynq across the design points. Overall, intra kernel parallelism has the lowest utilization except for LUT as memory. In intra kernel parallelism, the 2D-line buffers are not mapped directly to BRAMs but instead to LUTs do to the extra Read ports need. Although overall intra kernel parallelism performs best for the first layer in SqueezNet, the remaining layers would map to better utilize different forms of parallelism with respect to their inter and intra kernel data sharing patterns which are directly driven from the network topology.

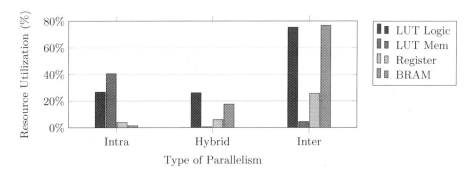

Fig. 16. Relative resource utilization on Xilinx Zynq across design points

5.3 System-Level Impact

In this part, we quantify the system-level benefits of the computing the first two layers on the edge node. Figure 17 compares two scenarios: (1) computing entire network on the edge server and (2) computing across the edge node and edge server (edge-node+edge-server). Figure 17b compares the execution time. Overall, the server+node cooperative computation achieves 32% improvement in the performance. Figure 17a compares the network communication traffic. Node+server cooperative computation reduces the communication and network traffic by more then 3x.

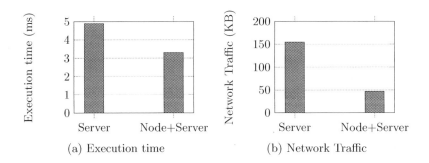

(a) Execution time   (b) Network Traffic

Fig. 17. Network traffic and execution time comparison between edge-server, and edge-node+edge-server scenarios

5.4 Comparison Against GPUs

This section is the alternative solution comparison, which compares our proposed architecture (implemented on Zynq FPGA) against the state of the art mobile GPU, Nvidia Jestosn TX2 [26]. Figure 18 compares both execution time (as the latency for performing single frame), and power consumption in the logarithmic scale. Figure 18a shows that our architecture (implemented on Zynq FPGA) has a latency cost of 0.24 ms. While the mobile GPU solution imposes a latency of 31.4 ms. Figure 18b shows that our proposed architecture can offer considerably lower power consumption over mobile GPUs. For execution 30 frames at the resolution of 227×227, GPU consumes 7.5 W. In contrast, our proposed architecture, implemented on Zynq FPGA, only consumes 0.315 W.

Our proposed architecture consumes about 24x lower power compared to Nvidia Jetson TX2 GPU, while imposing 130x less latency. Our proposed architecture is a data-flow machine, thus it only operates when the streaming pixels of the new frame are available. It is able to process the entire frame at 0.24 ms. It then stays in the standby mode until it receives the next frame streaming data. As a result, our architecture is able to even perform real-time processing at the much higher frame rates such as 60 fps and 120 fps.

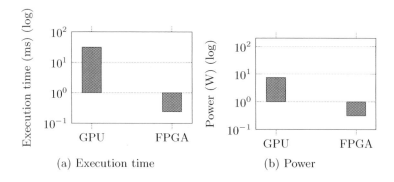

(a) Execution time   (b) Power

Fig. 18. Power and performance comparison against Nvidia Tegra TX2 GPU

6   Conclusions

In conclusion, this paper proposed a novel architecture template for real-time low-power execution of Convolutional Neural Networks at the edge. The proposed architecture is primarily targeted for FPGAs, and is able to offer configurable macro-pipeline datapath for scalable direct convolutions over streaming pixels. The proposed architecture is an example of a hybrid solution across edge nodes and edge servers for realizing compute-intensive deep learning applications. The proposed architecture is able to reduce the network traffic and execution time of the overall application. At the same time, it maintains the flexibility to map to any standard CNN network topology. Future work includes supporting full network topology acceleration on edge and supporting nonstandard CNN, as well as a workflow for mapping them efficiently to different FPGA boards.

References

1. Egmont-Petersen, M., de Ridder, D., Handels, H.: Image processing with neural networksa review. Pattern Recogn. **35**(10), 2279–2301 (2002)
2. Ciregan, D., Meier, U., Schmidhuber, J.: Multi-column deep neural networks for image classification. In: 2012 IEEE conference on Computer vision and pattern recognition (CVPR), pp. 3642–3649. IEEE (2012)
3. Collobert, R., Weston, J.: A unified architecture for natural language processing: deep neural networks with multitask learning. In: Proceedings of the 25th International Conference on Machine learning, pp. 160–167. ACM (2008)
4. Zhao, H., Wang, J., Gao, P.: A deep learning approach for condition-based, p. 32. STIoT Editorial Board (2017)
5. Paine, T., Jin, H., Yang, J., Lin, Z., Huang, T.: GPU asynchronous stochastic gradient descent to speed up neural network training. arXiv preprint arXiv:1312.6186 (2013)
6. Du, L., Du, Y., Li, Y., Su, J., Kuan, Y.C., Liu, C.C., Chang, M.C.F.: A reconfigurable streaming deep convolutional neural network accelerator for internet of things. IEEE Trans. Circ. Syst. I Reg. Pap. **65**(1), 198–208 (2018)
7. Wu, Y., Schuster, M., Chen, Z., Le, Q.V., Norouzi, M., Macherey, W., Krikun, M., Cao, Y., Gao, Q., Macherey, K., et al.: Google's neural machine translation system: bridging the gap between human and machine translation. arXiv preprint arXiv:1609.08144 (2016)
8. Microsoft brainwave. https://www.microsoft.com/en-us/research/blog/microsoft-unveils-project-brainwave/
9. Iandola, F.N., Han, S., Moskewicz, M.W., Ashraf, K., Dally, W.J., Keutzer, K.: Squeezenet: AlexNet-level accuracy with 50x fewer parameters and <0.5 mb model size. arXiv preprint arXiv:1602.07360 (2016)
10. Strigl, D., Kofler, K., Podlipnig, S.: Performance and scalability of GPU-based convolutional neural networks. In: 2010 18th Euromicro International Conference on Parallel, Distributed and Network-Based Processing (PDP), pp. 317–324. IEEE (2010)
11. Potluri, S., Fasih, A., Vutukuru, L.K., Al Machot, F., Kyamakya, K.: CNN based high performance computing for real time image processing on GPU. In: 2011 Joint 3rd International Workshop on Nonlinear Dynamics and Synchronization (INDS) and16th International Symposium on Theoretical Electrical Engineering (ISTET), pp. 1–7. IEEE (2011)
12. Nasse, F., Thurau, C., Fink, G.A.: Face detection using GPU-based convolutional neural networks. In: Jiang, X., Petkov, N. (eds.) CAIP 2009. LNCS, vol. 5702, pp. 83–90. Springer, Heidelberg (2009). https://doi.org/10.1007/978-3-642-03767-2_10
13. Latifi Oskouei, S.S., Golestani, H., Hashemi, M., Ghiasi, S.: CNNdroid: GPU-accelerated execution of trained deep convolutional neural networks on Android. In: Proceedings of the 2016 ACM on Multimedia Conference, pp. 1201–1205. ACM (2016)
14. Nagy, Z., Szolgay, P.: Configurable multilayer CNN-UM emulator on FPGA. IEEE Trans. Circ. Syst. I Fundam. Theory Appl. **50**(6), 774–778 (2003)
15. Tann, H., Hashemi, S., Bahar, R.I., Reda, S.: Hardware-software codesign of accurate, multiplier-free deep neural networks. In: 2017 54th ACM/EDAC/IEEE Design Automation Conference (DAC), pp. 1–6. IEEE (2017)

16. Sharma, H., Park, J., Mahajan, D., Amaro, E., Kim, J.K., Shao, C., Mishra, A., Esmaeilzadeh, H.: From high-level deep neural models to FPGAs. In: 2016 49th Annual IEEE/ACM International Symposium on Microarchitecture (MICRO), pp. 1–12. IEEE (2016)
17. Du, Z., Fasthuber, R., Chen, T., Ienne, P., Li, L., Luo, T., Feng, X., Chen, Y., Temam, O.: ShiDianNao: shifting vision processing closer to the sensor. In: ACM SIGARCH Computer Architecture News, vol. 43, pp. 92–104. ACM (2015)
18. Aimar, A., Mostafa, H., Calabrese, E., Rios-Navarro, A., Tapiador-Morales, R., Lungu, I.A., Milde, M.B., Corradi, F., Linares-Barranco, A., Liu, S.C., et al.: Null-Hop: a flexible convolutional neural network accelerator based on sparse representations of feature maps. arXiv preprint arXiv:1706.01406 (2017)
19. Han, S., Liu, X., Mao, H., Pu, J., Pedram, A., Horowitz, M.A., Dally, W.J.: EIE: efficient inference engine on compressed deep neural network. In: 2016 ACM/IEEE 43rd Annual International Symposium on Computer Architecture (ISCA), pp. 243–254. IEEE (2016)
20. Jafri, S.M.A.H., Hemani, A., Paul, K., Abbas, N.: MOCHA: morphable locality and compression aware architecture for convolutional neural networks. In: 2017 IEEE International Parallel and Distributed Processing Symposium (IPDPS), pp. 276–286. IEEE (2017)
21. Qadeer, W., Hameed, R., Shacham, O., Venkatesan, P., Kozyrakis, C., Horowitz, M.: Convolution engine: balancing efficiency and flexibility in specialized computing. Commun. ACM **58**(4), 85–93 (2015)
22. Alwani, M., Chen, H., Ferdman, M., Milder, P.: Fused-layer CNN accelerators. In: 2016 49th Annual IEEE/ACM International Symposium on Microarchitecture (MICRO), pp. 1–12. IEEE (2016)
23. Xu, L., Pham, K.D., Kim, H., Shi, W., Suh, T.: End-to-end big data processing protection in cloud environment using black boxes-an FPGA approach. Int. J. Cloud Comput. **2**, 14–27 (2014)
24. APU, A.P.U.: Zynq-7000 all programmable soc overview (2012)
25. Bachrach, J., Vo, H., Richards, B., Lee, Y., Waterman, A., Avižienis, R., Wawrzynek, J., Asanović, K.: Chisel: constructing hardware in a scala embedded language. In: Proceedings of the 49th Annual Design Automation Conference, pp. 1216–1225. ACM (2012)
26. Naphade, M., Anastasiu, D.C., Sharma, A., Jagrlamudi, V., Jeon, H., Liu, K., Chang, M.C., Lyu, S., Gao, Z.: The NVIDIA AI city challenge. In: IEEE Smart-World, Ubiquitous Intelligence and Computing, Advanced and Trusted Computed, Scalable Computing and Communications, Cloud and Big Data Computing, Internet of People and Smart City Innovation (SmartWorld/SCALCOM/UIC/ATC/CBDCom/IOP/SCI) (2017)

Application and Industry Track

Efficient Bare Metal Auto-scaling for NFV in Edge Computing

Xudong Pang, Jing Wang, Jingyu Wang, Qi Qi[✉], Jie Xu, and Zhenguang Yu

State Key Laboratory of Networking and Switching Technology,
Beijing University of Posts and Telecommunications, Beijing, China
qiqi8266@bupt.edu.cn

Abstract. Elasticity is an essential attribute of cloud data center, which is critical for operating resources in face of peaks and valleys of business. At present, the automatic scaling technique of virtual machines is widely studied, but barely for physical machines. Despite lack of flexibility, we all know that physical server can perform faster and more efficiently than virtualized instances, especially in Network Function Virtualization (NFV) systems. Some virtual network functions (VNFs) actually require high performance computing, which is a hard task for virtual machines. Besides, good management of bare metal resources can be significant for the data center power cost and human maintenance cost. Accordingly, we think that auto-scaling of physical machine is worth studying. This paper proposes a bare metal automatic scaling scheme based on workload prediction, and finally make tests on an open source NFV platform. The new scheme obtains good result on computation intensive VNFs scenario, including complete the scale in minutes, guarantee for the continuity of VNF processing business, and can cope with the load fluctuation better.

Keywords: Bare metal · NFV · Auto-scaling · Scheduling · Edge computing

1 Introduction

MEC offers storage and computational resources at the edge, reducing latency for mobile end users and utilizing more efficiently the mobile backhaul and core networks.

Network Function Virtualization (NFV) will leverage modern technologies such as those developed for cloud computing, which provides an analysis of the MEC orchestration considering standalone services, service mobility, joint network and service optimization as well as a comprehensive study of current orchestrator deployment options. That is to say there is always an edge data center behind the NFV system [1], and this kind of cloud data center usually consists of several servers, the workload time series for the whole cluster appear to be large fluctuation. Only auto-scaling of virtual machines cannot meet the needs of all. Some specific use-cases, for example, in the high-performance computing clusters, computing tasks that require access to hardware devices which cannot be virtualized [2], and for the database hosting (some databases run poorly in a hypervisor), single tenant dedicated hardware for performance, security, dependability and other regulatory requirements. When the cloud infrastructure rapidly

© Springer International Publishing AG, part of Springer Nature 2018
S. Liu et al. (Eds.): EDGE 2018, LNCS 10973, pp. 67–79, 2018.
https://doi.org/10.1007/978-3-319-94340-4_5

deployment, it's necessary for auto-scaling of bare metal resources. But managing that large number of physical servers is a hassle, if all by human operations, to ensure the quality of service (QoS) is an obvious challenge. Cloud computing itself has the characteristics of independent, safe, reliable, elastic, durable and others, so the automatic scaling of bare-metal resources is necessary.

Amazon Web Services (AWS) developed the first virtual machine auto-scaling tech in the industry, which is a solution for the holiday's 5 times shopping rush to normal flow. Moreover, the automatic scaling technique was applied to more areas, such as some of the virtualization resources of cloud computing. Accordingly, we consider how to make the bare-metal resources become more elastic for the ever-expanding data center. Traditional redundancy allocation can cause wasting of resources, so the main thing to do is to narrow the gap between allocating resources and actual needs.

However, there is no unified operating platform for bare metals currently, and we can only manage through some access and configuration tools such as IPMI, Cobbler or Ansible. Moreover, making all these processes automated is not easy, which requires a complete and elaborate workflow to complete, including new machines discovery, nodes deployment, as well as balance workloads to new online machines.

Besides, in advance allocation of resources can greatly improve quality and reduce the response latency of applications. Therefore, it is critical to find resource bottlenecks in time. We adopt Zabbix [3, 4] as a monitor, which is powerful and easy to expand. A recent survey classifies auto-scaling techniques into several major categories [5], including static policies, threshold-based polices, reinforcement learning, control theory and time-series analysis. For our design, we combine threshold rules and time-series analysis to make a suitable auto-scaling schedule algorithm. Based on the above techniques, we present an automatic horizontal scaling [6] algorithm for bare metal resources and made a series of experiments on this.

The second section introduces our related work. The third section describes details of our design framework, including core algorithm and related platform configurations. The fourth section describes detailed experiment steps and data comparisons. Finally, we conclude at the fifth section.

2   Related Work

NIST explained "rapid elasticity" as "capabilities can be elastically provisioned and released, in some cases automatically, to scale rapidly outward and inward commensurate with demand" [7]. The purpose of elasticity as defined in [8] is to provide performance, cost, increase infrastructure capacity, energy. All of these can be related to user load.

Due to the elasticity demand of physical server resources on NFV system, this paper probes into the automatic scaling of the bare metal resources. Here we use OpenStack [9] powered cloud as NFV infrastructure. It is well-known that OpenStack is an open source cloud platform, which has an excellent distributed architecture. A normal OpenStack cluster can be divided into the control nodes, network nodes, computing nodes, storage nodes. And there is also an Ironic project, which can help us manage bare metal resources. Better is, there is also a Tacker [10] project, which provide a NFV MANO conception implementations.

In addition, among many monitors we choose Zabbix, not only because it is one of the main monitoring tools of today's operation and maintenance staffs, but also its easy extendibility. Based on monitoring health status of cluster hardware, Zabbix can also make the upper application quality check, which feedback VNF response latency in time. Besides, Zabbix can also automatically discover and register new nodes. We use custom monitoring strategies, which are more suitable for both bare metal and NFV scenarios. In order to ensure the stability and smoothness of the upper services, Zabbix collects monitoring data periodically, which can be used to identify obvious features and predict loads of next moment.

We also present an auto scaling algorithm, which fully consider characteristics of bare metal resources, and also make full use of historical workload data for prediction. All these enable clusters to save as much resources as possible. Due to the process of bare metal provision is very time consuming, we need to do a good job in multi-stage pretreatment in advance, for example, packaging VNF image in advance, making some buffered servers, all these can make the new machine launch for work faster.

3 Architecture Design

3.1 Workflow of the Framework

Figure 1 shows our workflow, which based on a NFV Management and Orchestration (MANO) framework. The right part of this figure is a user request process, user requests which hit the same ASG will be dispatched to different servers by a load balancer.

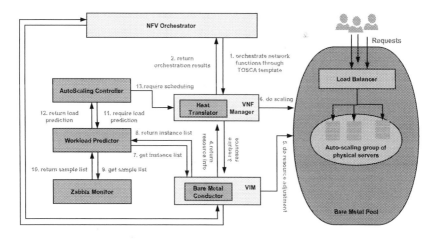

Fig. 1. Bare metal auto-scaling workflow on NFV MANO platform

Workload predictor uses historical data collected by Zabbix monitor as input sample, to make a workload prediction with our model, and then outputs a predict workload for next moment. This prediction will be send to auto-scaling controller, which will make a schedule decision with our design policy and send to VNF Manager (VNFM). VNFM is responsible for the lifecycle management of VNF. A VNF Manager can manage one or more VNFs, this is the ability to automate VNF including deployment, expansion, scaling, offline. VNFM can receive TOSCA templates from Orchestrator and transform them to VIM-understood profiles, and then handle bare metal instances though those profiles.

Topology and Orchestration Specification for Cloud Applications (TOSCA) is a service modeling language which can be used to model and deploy service function chains (SFCs). By defining TOSCA templates, which can be instantiated using concrete types, here we use this template to define VNF profiles. Orchestrator is responsible for NFV resources and is the basis of the upper software resource arrangement and management, this arrangement ability can be flexible adjustment of the VNF instances according to the requirements of the business. It's the core of the automatic ability.

Virtualized Infrastructure Manager (VIM) is a cloud platform, which is responsible for physical and virtual resource management. It can manage infrastructure resources, and schedule servers to different regions. Besides, our bare metal conductor will handle scaling actions in time.

3.2 Bare Metal Provision

According to our design, there are mainly three stages on bare metal provision, basically are as follows:

Machine Discovery: SNMP or INTEL RSA can be used to discover new electrically charged bare metals and report their information to conductor. Also, zero-conf provides a really good alternative for general bare metal discovery scenario, which does not rely on dedicated switches.

OS Installation: Nova uses Ironic driver to install operating system for the bare metals, and the images are provided by OpenStack glance service. This process is also the most time-consuming phase, average requiring approximately 20 min.

Software Configuration: Here we use tools like Ansible, Chef and puppet. Due to the new launched node will report its metadata to the controller voluntarily, and then automatically register to the corresponding cluster. We configure Zabbix agent and some service synchronize operations.

3.3 Monitor Configuration

Zabbix makes a good monitor for cloud data center, it is competent for large-scale cluster, can support IPMI and network equipment monitoring, besides, it is easy to extend, which is very suitable for NFV platform. According to [11], CPU accounts for 60% of the host's power consumption, and can basically represent machine energy consumption. We also use CPU load as default workload. Workloads of each processor can be detected by Zabbix agent periodically. Here we configure our Zabbix monitoring items: average CPU load of each physical server, average response latency of each VNF, and Power status of each physical server.

In Eq. (1), we define the workload of an ASG is the sum of workload of every processor in it.

$$Load(t) = \sum_{i=1}^{m} Load(t, i) * CoreNum(t, i) \qquad (1)$$

Another monitoring item is used to reflect the real-time service quality of VNFs. In Eq. (2), we define the average VNF responding latency of an ASG is the average latency of VNFs on every active server in the same group.

$$Latency(t) = \left. \sum_{i=1}^{m} Latency(t, i) \right/ m \qquad (2)$$

Auto-Registration: when a new machine is in the provision stage, it will be configured with a Zabbix agent, this agent can then be found by Zabbix server in local area, and then the machine will be registered to the corresponding auto-scaling group (ASG).

3.4 Workload Prediction Model

There are many forecasting models currently, including time series model, differential equation model, gray prediction model and so on. Differential equation model is based on the assumption of local rule independence, and the solution of it is difficult to obtain. And gray prediction model can be highlighted only when its prediction sequence has an exponential growth characteristic.

We choose autoregressive and moving average (ARMA) model [12], a time series prediction model, to predict the workloads of ASGs, and then convert to the schedule of bare-metal resources by schedule program.

In Eq. (3), we show an AR (3) as special shape, which is using a linear combination of the workloads of the previous three moments, to describe the workload predictions for the next moment. This equation is a result of what we screened through experiments (Fig. 2).

$$Load_{pre}(t + 1) = 0.8Load(t) + 0.15Load(t - 1) + 0.05Load(t - 2) \qquad (3)$$

$$Load_{pre}(t + 1) = 0.5Load(t) + \cdots + 0.5^{t}Load(1) \qquad (4)$$

Exponential smoothing prediction model is a special weighted moving average method, [13] which predicts the future workload by assigning a larger weight to the workload near the forecast period and making the weight from the near-far-decreasing exponential law. In Eq. (4), the mathematical expression of is shown in Table 1.

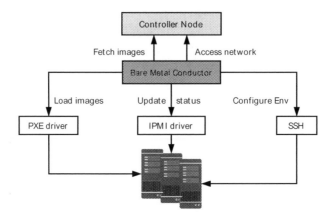

Fig. 2. Bare metal provision

Table 1. Related symbols and descriptions

Parameters	Meanings
m	Running server number of an ASG
n	Shutdown server number of an ASG
k	Total prediction times of an ASG
$Load(t,i)$	Average load of server i at time t
$Load(t)$	Predict average load of an ASG at time t
$Load_{avg}(t)$	Predict total load of an ASG at time t
$Load_{pre}(t)$	Predict total load of an ASG at time t
$CoreNum(t,i)$	Core number of running server i at time t
$CoreNum_{off}(t,j)$	Core number of an off-server j at time t
$CoreNum(t)$	Working processor number of an ASG at time t
$CoreNum_{min}(t)$	Min predict core number of an ASG at time t
$CoreNum_{max}(t)$	Max predict core number of an ASG at time t
$Latency(t,i)$	Average VNF response latency of server i
$Latency(t)$	Average VNF response latency of an ASG
$MinLoad$	Low average load threshold of an ASG
$MaxLoad$	High average load threshold of an ASG

Mean Absolute Error (MAE), Mean Square Error (MSE) and Mean Absolute Percent Error (MAPE) are three models usually used to evaluate prediction accuracy. The smaller obtained result is, the more accurate the prediction is. In this paper, we use MSE method to achieve better prediction accuracy, and Eq. (5) shows its mathematical expression.

$$MSE = \sqrt{\sum_{t=1}^{k} [Load_{pre}(t) - Load(t)]^2 \Big/ k} \qquad (5)$$

Table 2 shows the workload prediction MSE of Eqs. (3) and (4). We have a one-week statistical analysis of the load data and forecast data from our testbed. Comparing their mean squared errors of the two models, we can see that both models got good experiment results, and especially, the AR model obtained better prediction accuracy and is more stable.

Table 2. Mean squared error of prediction models

	Sun	Mon	Tue	Wen	Thu	Fri	Sat
AR	0.081	0.079	0.120	0.083	0.181	0.168	0.125
MA	0.102	0.092	0.107	0.101	0.239	0.156	0.164

3.5 Auto-Scaling Control Logic

First, we consider scale in and scale out as the following ways, that's a little bit different from usually on virtual machines.

Scale-out: when VNFM triggers scale out for an ASG, according to the need to increase the number of servers, first to find are the configured but shutdown servers in the same group, power them up to fit the need. But if no enough off machines left, it will then request for filling the gaps in demand by triggering provision process of bare metal in the resource pool. **Scale-in:** when VNFM triggers scale in action, it just chooses the right nodes and turn them off.

Notice that here requires all VNFs should be either a stateless type or can be automatically migrated. Stateless VNFs use a shared data layer, so they don't need to manage their own data. This is much easier and can be easily switched to meet the changing requirements [14].

In fact, the bare metal pool has a garbage collection mechanism. When there is not enough resource in it, it will find some shutdown servers in ASGs by Least Recently Used (LRU) policy [15] and then reset PXE as the first boot device.

In the Fig. 3, there are 3 statuses for a bare metal, those are UP, DOWN and EMPTY, which represent the basic status of active, shutdown, and released. Besides, there are generally 4 actions for a bare metal, those are ON, OFF, DEPLOY and RELEASE. Due to the DEPLOY action is very time-consuming, scale out always try to trigger ON action at first, but if there is no resource in ASG, it will request from bare metal pool, and DEPLOY new instances. Based on the above rules, a practical workflow carried out in stages. That is about how to deal with specific overload and low load.

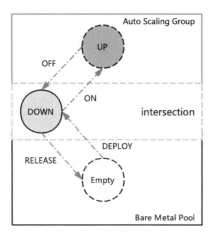

Fig. 3. State transition diagram of a bare metal

Stage One: real-time acquisition of prediction samples from Zabbix's monitoring data. Workload predictor will retrieve sample data every 30 min (according to physical machine acceptable interval, also avoid fluctuations). We use data of latest previous p moments as input, and output predict results of next moment [16]. Equation (3) describes a predict workload, it's the sum of all processor workloads in an ASG.

Stage Two: in this threshold judgment phase, according to the real-time load of each server, when the average load of an ASG occurs overload or low load situation, that ASG needs to be expanded or constrained according to its current state. We use the predict workload to adjust the number of working processors, according to Eq. (6) we can get the average value of predict load at time $t + 1$. Equations (7) and (8) shows the range of predict processor num. In Eq. (9) shows that conditions whether we need to adjust core number or not. We take the ideal situation, where MinLoad equals 0.75, MaxLoad equals 1.75.

$$Load_{avg}(t + 1) = Load_{pre}(t + 1) / CoreNum(t) \tag{6}$$

$$CoreNum_{min}(t + 1) = Load_{pre}(t + 1) / MaxLoad \tag{7}$$

$$CoreNum_{max}(t + 1) = Load_{pre}(t + 1) / MinLoad \tag{8}$$

$$CoreNum_{min}(t + 1) \le CoreNum(t) \le CoreNum_{max}(t + 1) \tag{9}$$

Stage Three: Scaling decision phase, when the condition described by inequality (9) is not satisfied, there should be an adjustment of that ASG. if the right condition of the inequality is not satisfied, that is, the ASG will be in a low load state and current resources will exceed real needs. The target of the processor resource to be adjusted is the result shown in the formula (8), the surplus processor quantity is the result shown in formula (10). Similarly, if the condition of the left side of the inequality is not satisfied, that is, the ASG will be in an over load state and current resources will do not meet real needs.

The target of the processor resource to be adjusted is the result shown in formula (7), insufficient core number is the result shown in formula (11).

$$\Delta_{lowload} = CoreNum_{\max}(t + 1) - CoreNum(t) \tag{10}$$

$$\Delta_{overload} = CoreNum_{\min}(t + 1) - CoreNum(t) \tag{11}$$

$$SORT([CoreNum(t, 1), \dots , CoreNum(t, i), \dots CoreNum(t, m)], ASC) \tag{12}$$

$$SORT([CoreNum_{off}(t, 1), \dots , CoreNum_{off}(t, j), \dots , CoreNum_{off}(t, n)], DESC) \tag{13}$$

Stage Four: in scheduling phase, the method of sorting allocation is adopted. If it will be in low load state, running servers in that ASG will be sorted by core number in ascending order according to formula (12), and the servers are selected sequentially until selected core number satisfies the result shown in formula (10). However, if it will be in overload state, off servers in that ASG will be sorted by core number in descending order according to formula (13), and the servers are selected sequentially until selected core number meets the result shown in formula (11). When the result cannot be satisfied, requests of remaining amount should be sending to the bare metal pool. Similarly, do sorting for bare metals according to formula (13), and select bare metals sequentially until it meets the demand, if resources in bare metal pool still cannot meet needs, then alert for datacenter resource shortage and wait for free resources in queue.

4   Implementation and Evaluation

Experiment should be in real production environment, the biggest advantage of this is we can validate the stability. But in order to avoid the experiment cost and in a more controlled environment, we decided to setup a customized test bed, this will cost some effort on system configuration.

In this platform, we used ten physical servers to test and optimize our auto-scaling algorithm. Each physical machine has 12 Intel® Core CPUs, 24 GB RAM and 10G Ethernet, and powered with CentOS7 system. There are two active nodes at initialization phase, one controller and network node, one compute.

In this paper we use Deep Packet Inspection (DPI) as the experimental VNF, for it's a computation intensive network function and this is a typical bare metal scenario. Figure 4 shows our measuring method, we use a client program to send requests to a flow receiver and measure the response latency difference between closing and opening the DPI firewall [17]. We wrote about 2 thousand lines of code (RScript and Python) for this test bed, including prediction algorithms, auto-scaling control and automation combination logic.

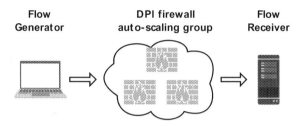

Fig. 4. DPI performance test

We compare the actual performance of multiple scheduling algorithms, assessing the VNF response rate and the number of physical servers used. Three schedule algorithms are chosen as the evaluation benchmarks. The four schedulers prediction-based and with transition state, no-prediction but with transition state, prediction-based but with no transition state, and no-prediction and with no transition state, represent four different scaling strategies are denoted by s1, s2, s3 and s4, respectively.

The performance of these schedulers is evaluated mainly from two perspectives, eager mode and idle mode, which represent two extremes that can highlight our auto-scaling policies. For the sake of statement, here we define the request density from 0 to 1, meaning density increasing.

First, we show a more comprehensive perspective (from idle mode to eager mode) in Fig. 5. Each point represents the average workload per processor. We can see that the CPU loads trend of our proposed auto-scaling scheme is more stable and is the case of the smallest fluctuations.

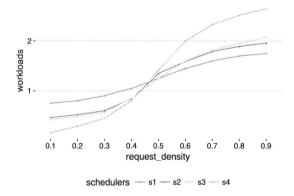

Fig. 5. Average workloads per processor

Figure 6 shows that when bare metal resources are insufficient, requests can be delayed due to the high CPU loads. We can see that s2 and s3 show roughly the same performance. And our strategy is about 18% less than their average delay. As for the no-prediction and no transition state scheduler, our strategy is about 29% less than the average delay. The conclusion is our prediction-based auto-scaling scheme can improve the quality of service VNF under eager mode.

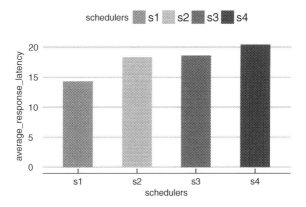

Fig. 6. Average VNF latency for eager mode (ms)

Figure 7 shows that when the bare metal resources are sufficient, power resources may be wasted, due to the adjustment is not timely. We can see that s2 and s3 generally use the same number of servers, about wasted 16% processor resources than our scheduler. Moreover, the no prediction and no transition state scheduler wasted about 21% of the power resources than ours. The conclusion is our prediction-based auto-scaling scheme can reduce power waste under idle mode.

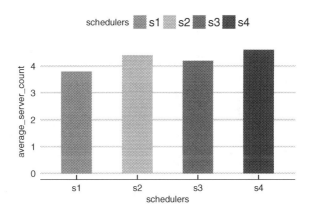

Fig. 7. Average server counts for idle mode

5 Conclusion

In this paper, we presented a bare metal auto scaling mechanism based on NFV system. This mechanism uses a method of forecasting and pre-allocating physical resources, to make VNFs scale in and scale out more smoothly. Compared with traditional way of relying more on human operations, it provides better QoS. Our work on bare metal auto-scaling may provide an idea for the NFV platform maintenance, with more intelligent, green, tight performance. Using this method, we believe that we opened a door for bare metal auto-scaling to obtain significant improvements in both cost and execution time. As the future work we intend to extend the prediction algorithm optimization, there is still great room for improvement. And we also want to study on the auto-scaling supporting both virtual machine and physical hosts, in a hybrid mode. This may be a more normal scenario in practice. In the future, the NFV resource scaling may can be optimized by the popular machine learning mechanisms [18–21].

Acknowledgment. This work was jointly supported by: (1) National Natural Science Foundation of China (No. 61771068, 61671079, 61471063, 61372120, 61421061); (2) Beijing Municipal Natural Science Foundation (No. 4182041, 4152039); (3) the National Basic Research Program of China (No. 2013CB329102).

References

1. ETSI: Network Functions Virtualisation (2012). https://portal.etsi.org/nfv/nfvwhitepaper.pdf
2. Gupta, A., Kale, L.V., Milojicic, D., Faraboschi, P., Balle, S.M.: HPC-aware VM placement in infrastructure clouds. In: Cloud Engineering (IC2E) (2013)
3. Naik, P., Shaw, D.K., Vutukuru, M.: NFVPerf: online performance monitoring and bottleneck detection for NFV. In: Network Function Virtualization and Software Defined Networks (NFV-SDN), 7–10 November 2016
4. Managing and monitoring performance in SDN/NFV (2015). https://www.virtualizationpractice.com/managing-monitoring-performance-sdn-nfv-32088/. Accessed 15 Dec 2015
5. Gajjar, P., Shah, B.: An efficient scalable framework for auto scaling services in cloud computing environment. IJIRT **2**, 113–120 (2016)
6. Chaloemwat, W., Kitisin, S.: Horizontal auto-scaling and process migration mechanism for cloud services with skewness algorithm. In: International Joint Conference on Computer Science and Software Engineering (2016)
7. Mell, P., Grance, T.: The NIST definition of cloud computing (2011)
8. Sakellariou, R., Zhao, H.: A hybrid heuristic for dag scheduling on heterogeneous systems. In: 18th IEEE International Parallel and Distributed Processing Symposium (2004)
9. OpenStack (2010). https://www.openstack.org/
10. Tacker (2015). https://wiki.openstack.org/wiki/Tacker
11. Fan, X., Weber, W.D., Barroso, L.A.: Power provisioning for a warehouse-sized computer. ACM SIGARCH Comput. Architect. News **35**(2), 13–23 (2007)
12. Wu, Y., Hwang, K., Yuan, Y., Zheng, W.: Adaptive workload prediction of grid performance in confidence windows. IEEE Trans. Parallel Distrib. Syst. **21**(7), 925–938 (2010)
13. Liang, W., Huang, T., Chen, J., Liu, Y.: Workload prediction-based algorithm for consolidation of virtual machines. J. Electron. Inf. Technol. **35**(6), 1271–1276 (2013)
14. Kablan, M., Caldwell, B., Han, R., Jamjoom, H., Keller, E.: Stateless network functions. In: SIGCOMM (2015)
15. Liu, C., Liu, Z., Zhang, D.: A cloud computing physical machine recovery method and its device. CN102831016 A (2012)
16. Chuprikov, P., Nikolenko, S., Kogan, K.: On demand elastic capacity planning for service auto-scaling. In: IEEE International Conference on Computer Communications (INFOCOM) (2016)
17. Garcia, J.: A clustering-based analysis of DPI-labeled videoflow characteristics in cellular networks. In: Integrated Network and Service Management (IM), 8–12 May 2017

18. Xu, P., Yin, Q., Huang, Y., Song, Y.-Z., Ma, Z., Wang, L., Xiang, T., Kleijn, W.B., Guo, J.: Cross-modal subspace learning for fine-grained sketch-based image retrieval. Neurocomputing **278**, 75–86 (2018)

19. Ma, Z., Xue, J.-H., Leijon, A., Tan, Z.-H., Yang, Z., Guo, J.: Decorrelation of neutral vector variables: theory and applications. IEEE Trans. Neural Netw. Learn. Syst. **29**(1), 129–143 (2018)

20. Liu, W., Cao, J., Yang, L., Xu, L., Qiu, X., Li, J.: AppBooster: boosting the performance of interactive mobile applications with computation offloading and parameter tuning. IEEE Trans. Parallel Distrib. Syst. **28**(6), 1593–1606 (2017)

21. Ma, Z., Rana, P.K., Taghia, J., Flierl, M., Leijon, A.: Bayesian estimation of dirichlet mixture model with variational inference. Pattern Recogn. **47**(9), 3143–3157 (2014)

Mobile Edge Offloading Using Markov Decision Processes

Khalid R. Alasmari[1], Robert C. Green II[2(✉)], and Mansoor Alam[1]

[1] EECS Department, The University of Toledo, Toledo, OH 43606, USA
Khalid.Al-Asmari@rockets.utoledo.edu, Mansoor.Alam2@utoledo.edu
[2] Department of Computer Science, Bowling Green State University,
Bowling Green, OH 43403, USA
greenr@bgsu.edu

Abstract. Considering where to process data and perform computation is becoming a more difficult problem as Mobile Edge Computing (MEC) and Mobile Cloud Computing (MCC) continue to evolve. In order to balance constraints and objectives regarding items like computation time and energy consumption, computation and data should be automatically shifted between mobile devices, the edge, and the cloud. To address this issue, this study proposes a Markov Decision Process (MDP) based methodology to intelligently make such choices while optimizing multiple objectives. Results demonstrate an 17.47% or greater increase in performance.

1 Introduction

Overall, the number of smart phone users is rapidly increasing. According to a Gartner press release from August 22, 2017 [1], Global sales of smart phones to end users totaled 366.2 million units in the second quarter of 2017, a 6.7% increase over the second quarter of 2016. These numbers demonstrate the higher demand for smart phones and their level of integration into everyday life. However, smart phones still face the challenge of performing complex multimedia operations such as image and video processing, object or face recognition, and augmented reality applications [2]. As many of these operations can be computationally intense, maintaining battery life while addressing a consumer's need is becoming a bigger challenge.

In [3], Running tasks on mobile device will consume a large amount of energy and bandwidth. Therefore, many researchers have proposed offloading mechanism to reduce energy consumption on mobile devices by moving all or some of the computation to the cloud [2,4]. Some of mobile applications, such as perception and multimedia applications, the network latency of the cloud might face a difficulty to achieve the desired performance [5]. Thus, mobiles devices may prefer to access edge servers that have a lower latency for computation offloading.

This study differs from previous studies by adding an edge device between the mobile device and the cloud servers to perform data processing at the edge of the

© Springer International Publishing AG, part of Springer Nature 2018
S. Liu et al. (Eds.): EDGE 2018, LNCS 10973, pp. 80–90, 2018.
https://doi.org/10.1007/978-3-319-94340-4_6

network rather than sending them towards the cloud. This reduces end-to-end delay, energy consumption and lower network congestion. Figure 1 illustrates an architecture of our proposed system model for multisite offloading that include a mobile device, cloud server and edge server. In this study, a methodology is proposed that shows the offload tasks to edge servers is the effective technique to save mobile device energy and reduce time delay. Therefore, we investigate the collaborative application execution between the mobile device, the edge servers and the cloud servers to conserve the energy consumption on the mobile device by offloading technique.

The rest of the paper is organized as follows. Section 2 provides the related work. Then in Sect. 3, a MDP methodology and formulation. Section 4 provides a numerical simulation and evaluation. Finally, Sect. 5 concludes this paper.

2   Related Work

There are a variety of previous works that exist in the area of multi-site offloading policies using Markov decision processes (MDPs) for mobile cloud computing. Terefe et al. [3] proposed a multisite offloading policy (MDP) for mobile devices in order to minimize energy consumption. The authors adopted a discrete time Markov chain (DTMC) to model a fading channel and applied a MDP framework to formulate the energy and time consumption of the multi-site offloading decisions problem. The authors proposed the Energy-efficient Multisite Offloading Policy (EMOP) algorithm with the value iteration algorithm (VIA) to determine the optimal policy for a Markov chain model. However, their work considers multiple cloud serves. The result shows that the EMOP algorithm is an efficient multisite computation offloading approach for mobile devices with respect to both energy consumption and execution time. Our approach considers edge computing to develop more efficient offloading solution in energy and time.

Nasseri et al. [6] proposed a methodology that allowed various computation tasks to be offloaded to mobile devices that belong to users considering battery life, response delay, and power consumption. The authors adopted MDP optimal policies and lookup tables for mobile cloud computing in order to guide mobile devices in accepting or rejecting requests based on rewards. Result showed higher rewards with a combination of a smaller delay in responding to a request and reduced power consumption. However, sending the mobile phones data to the lookup tables to update the battery level, signal strength and the distance to helper consumes more energy. In this paper, we consider offloading sites have own database server that could do the computational more easier and without spending time and energy to retrieve the information from another location.

Zhang et al., in [4], proposed a framework solution for energy-optimal mobile cloud computing under stochastic wireless channel. The authors adapted a dynamic configuring technique to the clock frequency of the chip in order to minimize the computation energy in mobile device. The authors also developed a formulation that leads to an optimal data transmission schedule across the stochastic wireless channel to minimize the transmission energy in cloud space.

The authors employ the two-state Markov model known as the Gilbert-Elliot channel. The result suggest offloading mobile applications to the cloud in order to save a significant amount of energy in some application. Our approach considers Markov decision processes (MDPs) with three channel states (mobile, edge and cloud).

3   MDP Methodology and Formulation

MDPs are used to help to make decisions in a stochastic environment. A MDP is a discrete time stochastic control process. It is defined by a state space for the system, an action space, a stochastic transition to determine how the system will move to next state, and a reward function which determines the immediate consequence for the agent's choice of action a while in state s. Hence, a Markov decision process can be defined by the 4-tuple (S, A, P, R) with the following meaning:

- S is a finite set of states,
- A is a finite set of actions,
- $P(s, s', a)$ is the probability that action a in state s at time t will lead to state s' at time $t + 1$,
- $R(s, s', a)$ is the immediate reward received after transition to state s' from state s with action a.

3.1   MDP Formulation

This section introduces the formulation of our Multisite offloading in mobile edge computing adapting the MDP methodology including appropriate policy constructs (i.e. state space, decision epochs, actions, transition probabilities, policy, and reward function). The system architecture is shown in Fig. 1. Algorithm 2 shows the Energy-efficient multisite offloading policy algorithm.

State Space. The state space, S is defined as $S = \{1, 2, 3\}$ where 1 denotes the mobile space, 2 denotes the Edge site 1 and 3 denotes the Cloud.

Decision Epochs and Actions. The decision epoch is represented as $T = \{0, 1, 2, \ldots, n, n + 1\}$ where decision epoch $t \in T$ indicates that component t has already executed.

Transition Probabilities. The transition probabilities play the role of the next-state function in a problem-solving search. Accordingly, for each state $s(t)$ and action $a(t)$, the probability that the next state will be $s(t + 1)$.

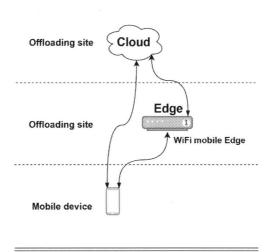

Fig. 1. System model for the multi-site offloading formulation.

Reward Function. The reward function in this study considers two components, Energy consumption and computation time, resulting in two objective functions, $R_e(s, a)$ and $R_t(s, a)$. Based on the reward function R and the transition function T_p, a transition is made to state s' with probability T_p and a reward $R(s, s', a)$ is received [7].

Value Iteration Algorithm. The VIA in Algorithm 1 will yield an approximation to the optimal value function and is used in this study.

Algorithm 1. Value Iteration Algorithm (VIA)

---

for all $s \in S$ **do** $V \leftarrow 0$
end for
repeat $\Delta \leftarrow 0$
    for all $s \in S$ **do**
    $v \leftarrow V(s)$
    $V(s) \leftarrow max_a \sum_{s'} P^a_{ss'}[R^a_{ss'} + \gamma V(s')]$
    $\Delta \leftarrow max\,(\Delta, |v - V(s)|)]$

    end for
until $\Delta \leq \theta($ a small positive number $)$
$\pi(s) \leftarrow argmax_a \sum_{s'} P^a_{ss'}[R^a_{ss'} + \gamma V(s')]$

---

4   Numerical Simulation and Evaluation

In this section, the performance of the proposed MDP-based methodology in terms of energy consumption and computation time is analyzed.

4.1   Simulation Setup

This study considers a scenario with two offloading sites (*i.e.*, $K = 2$). Site 1 simulates an edge server and Site 2 simulates a cloud server that also contains a database server as shown in Fig. 1. The mobile application consists of n components in a linear topology, where each component could migrate to one of the two offloading sites or remain on the mobile device in any given step. It is assumed that the two offloading sites have different computational capacity and network bandwidth [3].

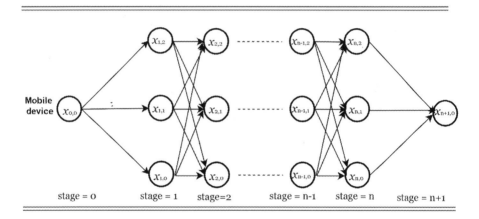

Fig. 2. State transitions in the MDP model.

In the proposed model, the decision epoch is represented as $T = \{0, 1, 2, \ldots, n, n + 1\}$, where decision epoch $t \in T$ indicates that component t has already executed. The decision maker chooses either the action taken where $a = 1$ (good) at time t that causes the state to transition to a new state at time $t + 1$ from the current state, or the action is not taken where $a = 0$ (bad) [3]. In that event, at the beginning of every stage, a decision-maker observes the current state, and chooses an action: migrate execution or continue execution, and receives a reward depending on the current state [8].

The system state at decision epoch t and $i \in [0,k]$ denotes the location of the executed component t. It is assumed that the executions start at the mobile device and the initial channel state is observed to be good, which means computation may be offloaded to one of the two sites. There are $n+2$ stages of execution considered, as shown in Fig. 2. Stage 0, at decision epoch 0, and stage $n+1$ represent the initiation and termination of application execution, respectively. In each stage, the system state is defined as $x_i = (t_i, \gamma_i)$ where t_i is the location of the executed component t, and γ_i is the channel state of the next time slot between the mobile and offloading sites (i.e., ether good or bad).

Since the application execution starts and ends on the mobile device, it also holds that $t_0 = 0$, and $t_{n+1} = 0$.

The execution sites are defined as $Q = \{q_0, q_1, q_2\}$, where q_0 represents the mobile device, q_1 denotes the offloading site 1 (edge server) and q_2 denotes the offloading site 2 (cloud server). Energy cost is defined as $E_v = \{e_{v_0}, e_{v_1}, e_{v_2}\}$, where e_{v_0}, e_{v_1} and e_{v_2} denotes the energy cost of component v that executed on offloading site q_0, q_1 and q_2, respectively. Time cost is defined as $T_v = \{t_{v_0}, t_{v_1}, t_{v_2}\}$, where t_{v_0}, t_{v_1} and t_{v_2} denotes the time cost to execute component v on each of the offloading sites q_0, q_1 and q_2, respectively [3].

f_0, f_1 and f_2 are defined as the CPU clock speeds (cycles/second) of mobile device q_0, offloading site 1 (q_1), and offloading site 2 (q_2). The total CPU cycles needed by the instructions of component v is W_v. $t_{v_i}^c$ denotes the computational time of executing component v on site q_i and is given by:

$$t_{v_i}^c = \frac{w_v}{f_i} \forall v \in V \text{ and } \forall i \in [0,k] \tag{1}$$

Data sent and received by component v as denoted as d_{v_s} and d_{v_r}, respectively. Since the database is located at the cloud site, r_0 and r_1 are defined as the data rate between site q_0 and site q_1 and the database server [3]. Also, $t_{v_i}^s$ and $t_{v_i}^r$ are defined as the communication time spent for sending and receiving data from the database by component v on site q_i, given by (2) and (3).

$$t_{v_i}^s = \frac{d_{v_s}}{r_i}, \forall v \in V \text{ and } \forall i \in [0,k] \tag{2}$$

$$t_{v_i}^r = \frac{d_{v_r}}{r_i}, \forall v \in V \text{ and } \forall i \in [0,k] \tag{3}$$

t_{v_i} is defined as the total time cost of component v on site q_i and is given by

$$t_{v_i} = t_{v_i}^c + t_{v_i}^s + t_{v_i}^r \tag{4}$$

It is assumed that the energy consumption E_v is calculated as the amount of energy a mobile device spends while executing the component or waiting for the component to be executed on offloading sites [3]. Energy cost of a component is then defined by e_{v_i} in (5) where p_c is the mobile power consumption when computing, p_s is the mobile power consumption when sending data, p_r is the mobile power consumption when receiving data, and p_{idle} is the Mobile power consumption at idle [3].

$$e_{v_i} = \begin{cases} t_{v_i}^c \times p_c + t_{v_i}^s \times p_s + t_{v_i}^r \times p_r, \\ t_{v_i} \times p_{idle} \end{cases} \tag{5}$$

The communication energy cost between two edges is denoted as $e_{u,v} = \{e_{u_0 v_0}, e_{u_0 v_1}, \ldots, e_{u_0 v_2}, e_{u_1 v_0}, \ldots, e_{u_2 v_2}\}$. (6) represents the communication energy spent on the edge for sending data from a mobile to an offloading site, either and edge server or cloud server where e_{u_i, v_j} denotes the energy cost if component u is executed on site q_i and component v is executed on site q_j, and t_{u_i, v_j} is the time spent transferring data from component u on site q_i to component v on site q_j [3].

$$e_{u_i, v_j} = t_{u_i, v_j} \times p_s, \forall (u, v) \in E \text{ and } i = 0, j \in [1, 2] \tag{6}$$

(7) represents the communication energy spent on the edge for receiving data from an offloading site either edge server or cloud server to a mobile device, given by

$$e_{u_i, v_j} = t_{u_i, v_j} \times p_r \forall (u, v) \in E, i \in [1, 2], j = 0 \tag{7}$$

The energy a mobile device spends while waiting for data transfer between components on different offloading sites is represented by (8) taking into consideration that $p_s > p_r > p_c > p_{idle}$ [9].

$$e_{u_i, v_j} = t_{u_i, v_j} \times p_{idle}, \forall (u, v) \in E, i, j \in [1, 2], i \neq j \tag{8}$$

The communication time spent to transfer data from component u on site q_i to component v on site q_j is denoted as t_{u_i, v_j} and is given by given by (9) where $d_{u,v}$ denotes the data transferred from component u to v, and $r_{i,j}$ denotes the transmission rate between sites q_i and q_j [3].

$$t_{u_i, v_j} = \frac{d_{u,v}}{r_{ij}}, \tag{9}$$

Algorithm 2. Energy-efficient multisite offloading policy algorithm

---

Input: *initialization*
Output: e_M,e_E,e_C,t_M,t_E,t_C

while Not at end of stages **do**
$R =< R_1, R_2, R_3 >$
$\quad\quad\quad\quad\quad\quad\quad\quad\quad\quad\quad\quad\quad$ ▷ TP_1 for action $a = 1$ mobile
$\quad\quad\quad\quad\quad\quad\quad\quad\quad\quad\quad\quad$ ▷ TP_2 for action $a = 2$ Edge and Cloud
$\quad\quad policy = floor(2 \times rand(1, N)) + 1$
$\quad\quad\quad\quad\quad\quad\quad$ ▷ Random vector of 1 (stay at mobile)and 2 (offloading)

$\quad\quad N \leftarrow 3$
$\quad\quad$ **for** i $= 1$ to N **do**
$\quad\quad\quad$ **for** j = 1 to N **do**
$\quad\quad\quad\quad$ TP(i,j) = T(i,j,policy(i))
$\quad\quad\quad$ **end for**
$\quad\quad$ **end for**
$\quad\quad converge \leftarrow 0$
$\quad\quad V_0 \leftarrow 0$
$\quad\quad \gamma \leftarrow 0.9$
$\quad\quad$ **while** converge **do**
$\quad\quad\quad V = transpose(R) + \gamma \times TP \times (transpose(V_0))$
$\quad\quad\quad old\_V \leftarrow V_0$
$\quad\quad\quad V_0 \leftarrow inverse(V)$
$\quad\quad\quad$ **if** abs(old_V - V_0) < 0.0001 **then**
$\quad\quad\quad\quad converge \leftarrow 1$
$\quad\quad\quad$ **end if**
$\quad\quad$ **end while**
$\quad\quad$ Return $< e_M, e_E, e_C, t_M, t_E, t_C >$

end while

4.2 Simulation Results

Table 1 shows the result of the multi-site offloading simulation using MDP. The simulation was run eight times for a differing number of nodes. In the first experiment where nodes or stages is equal to 5, two of the stages have executed at the mobile device, two have executed at the edge server, and one has executed at the cloud server. The total energy consumption of the mobile device is 19.25 J, the edge server consumes 2.19 J, and the cloud server consumes 0.801 J. As mentioned in a previous section, the execution starts and ends at the mobile device. Thus, there must be at least two stages executed at mobile device.

Several observations can be made when considering Tables 1, 2, 3 and 4. First, the energy consumption of executing an application on the edge server results in a larger energy saving than compared to the cloud server. Second, the time cost for multiple site execution of single edge and cloud nodes is less than the time cost for single mobile node, for example, when the nodes equal to 40, the average time cost for edge per node is 3.523 s, the average time cost for cloud per node is 3.839 s, and the average time cost for mobile per node is 10.6 s, as shown in Table 2. Third, the energy saving of executing an application across multiple sites (i.e., edge and cloud) is between 17.473%–46.27% of the energy consumption of execution on single site server (i.e., mobile device), as shown in Table 3. Moreover, we noticed that the energy saving percentage decreases as nodes increases, as shown in Table 3. However, the energy consumption of execution on a edge server is higher than a cloud server because the database is located at the cloud where there is a higher computational speed and faster access to a database, while the mobile device or edge servers have to make data requests to the cloud server. Fourth, the time cost for multiple site execution is less than the time cost for single site execution. The time cost for multiple site execution is between 41.88%–64.52% of the time cost of execution on single site server (i.e., mobile device), as shown in Table 4.

Table 1. Energy consumption of executing an application on multiple sites.

Node	No. of execution			Energy (J)		
	Mobile	Edge	Cloud	Mobile	Edge	Cloud
5	2	2	1	19.25	2.19	0.801
10	2	6	2	18.509	6.402	2.841
15	2	10	3	19.178	12.003	3.906
20	2	12	6	18.677	12.738	7.878
25	2	14	9	19.301	15.204	10.494
30	2	16	12	19.604	19.275	15.57
35	2	21	12	19.1999	24.983	13.011
40	2	24	14	18.077	30.906	16.125

Table 2. Time cost of executing an application on multiple sites.

Node	No. of execution			Time (sec.)		
	Mobile	Edge	Cloud	Mobile	Edge	Cloud
5	2	2	1	23.21	7.86	2.67
10	2	6	2	21.54	19.58	9.47
15	2	10	3	18.64	37.32	13.02
20	2	12	6	19.32	42.8	26.26
25	2	14	9	22.58	51.19	34.98
30	2	16	12	18.46	54.53	51.9
35	2	21	12	21.18	85.045	43.37
40	2	24	14	21.2	84.56	53.75

Table 3. Total energy consumption of executing an application on multiple sites and single site.

Node	Energy (J)		Energy saving (%)
	Multiple site	Single site	
5	22.241	48.065	46.27
10	27.752	93.781	29.59
15	35.087	144.126	24.34
20	39.293	190.541	20.62
25	44.999	235.441	19.11
30	54.449	284.622	19.13
35	57.1925	333.092	17.17
40	65.108	372.508	17.47

Table 4. Total time cost of executing an application on multiple sites and single site.

Node	Time (sec.)		Time saving (%)
	Multiple site	Single site	
5	33.74	52.29	64.52
10	50.59	99.94	50.62
15	68.98	149.13	46.25
20	88.38	199.68	44.26
25	108.75	251.2	43.29
30	124.79	298.39	42.83
35	149.595	353.82	42.27
40	169.51	404.71	41.88

5 Conclusion

This study has investigated the problem of how to save energy and time for mobile devices by executing some components of mobile applications remotely (e.g., on the edge server or in a cloud server). A MDP-based methodology was formulated to optimize energy consumption and execution time, resulting in savings of 17.47% to nearly 46.27%.

In the future, this work will be enhanced through multiple routes:

- Various algorithms and techniques like dynamic programming or ant colony optimization (ACO) may be compared with the MDP-based model in order to evaluate which algorithms perform best when optimizing computation time and energy consumption;
- The system may be expanded to be more realistic, involving multiple mobile devices, multiple edge servers, and a variety of a cloud servers leading to a more complex state space and more difficult optimization;

– Calculation of the MDP process may be varied from a centralized to a decentralized position, resulting in various impacts in optimization; and
– New reward functions, including the possible inclusion of some type of token/credit may be included [6].

References

1. van der Meulen, R., Forni, A.A.: Gartner says demand for 4G smartphones in emerging markets spurred growth in second quarter of 2017. Technical report, Gartner (2017)
2. Verbelen, T., Stevens, T., Simoens, P., Turck, F.D., Dhoedt, B.: Dynamic deployment and quality adaptation for mobile augmented reality applications. J. Syst. Softw. **84**(11), 1871–1882 (2011)
3. Terefe, M.B., Lee, H., Heo, N., Fox, G.C., Oh, S.: Energy-efficient multisite offloading policy using Markov decision process for mobile cloud computing. Pervasive Mob. Comput. **27**, 75–89 (2016)
4. Zhang, W., Wen, Y., Guan, K.: Energy-optimal mobile cloud computing under stochastic wireless channel. IEEE Trans. Wirel. Commun. **12**(9), 4569–4581 (2013)
5. Bahl, P., Han, R.Y., Li, L.E., Satyanarayanan, M.: Advancing the state of mobile cloud computing. In: Proceedings of the Third ACM Workshop on Mobile Cloud Computing and Services, MCS 2012, pp. 21–28. ACM, New York (2012)
6. Nasseri, M., Alam, M., Green, R.C.: MDP based optimal policy for collaborative processing using mobile cloud computing. In: IEEE 2nd International Conference on Cloud Networking (CloudNet), pp. 123–129 (2013)
7. van Otterlo, M.: Markov decision processes: concepts and algorithms, May 2009. Compiled for the SIKS Course on Learning and Reasoning
8. Bellman, R.: A Markovian decision process. Technical report, DTIC (1957)
9. Kumar, K., Lu, Y.H.: Cloud computing for mobile users: can offloading computation save energy? Computer **43**(4), 51–56 (2010)

A Face Recognition System Based on Cloud Computing and AI Edge for IOT

Junjie Zeng[1,2(✉)], Cheng Li[1,2], and Liang-Jie Zhang[1,2]

[1] National Engineering Research Center for Supporting Software of Enterprise Internet Services, Chengdu, China
junjiezeng87@gmail.com

[2] Kingdee Research, Kingdee International Software Group Company Limited, Shenzhen, China

Abstract. With the demand for interconnection of all things, more and more kinds of sensors are connected to the Internet of Things. Different from traditional sensors, such as low transmission frequency and small data volume, visual sensors have the characteristics of high transmission rate and large data volume. Vision sensors are widely used in security, health care and other face recognition. This paper proposes a combination of edge-based artificial intelligence and cloud computing that is suitable for areas such as face recognition and security that require a large number of visual sensors and image processing and analysis. In order to verify the effectiveness of the technical framework proposed in this paper, a complete demonstration system was built at the end of the paper based on the rk3288 and cloud server to prove the excellence of the system described in this paper.

Keywords: Face recognition system · AI Edge · IOT · Cloud computing

1   Introduction

At present, the Internet of Things is growing faster and faster. More and more types and quantities of IoT devices will be connected to the network. IoT can be viewed as a global infrastructure for the information society [1, 2]. Because of the numerous opportunities that IoT provides, the number of connected devices is increasing rapidly, and International Data Corporation (IDC) predicted that number to reach 29 billion by 2020 [3–5].

Among these growing IoT devices, in addition to traditional low-speed, small-data-rate sensor devices, some new types of IoT devices are gradually increasing, and vision sensor devices are among the more and more concerned types. The vision sensor is a general term for a series of image input devices, and the data it acquires are mostly still photos or dynamic videos. Benefiting from the development since they have abilities to recognize a person in the incorrect area and at the false hour because this person may be a bad person for the environment [12].

The system based on vision sensor is divided into two kinds of systems based on cloud processing and local processing according to the different ways of image processing. In a cloud-based system, the vision sensor collects the image data and

© Springer International Publishing AG, part of Springer Nature 2018
S. Liu et al. (Eds.): EDGE 2018, LNCS 10973, pp. 91–98, 2018.
https://doi.org/10.1007/978-3-319-94340-4_7

uploads it to the cloud service center for processing. In the local processing system, the image data obtained by the vision sensor will be processed in the local hardware system.

As shown in Fig. 1, the cloud-based face recognition system, the vision sensor uploads the obtained image data and waits for the cloud center to perform comparative analysis according to the image data. Its advantages are a simple structure, low cost on the equipment side, and can support different numbers of vision sensor devices according to the capabilities of the cloud computing center. However, because the image data needs to be uploaded through the network, although the image data can be reduced in size by a compression technique, it still suffers from a great deal of interference from the network state. When the network state is not ideal, the delay is very serious. And limited by the ability of the cloud computing center, when the number of visual sensors is huge, the computational expense of concurrent processing will be enormous of artificial intelligence technology, vision sensors are widely used in fields such as autopilot, security protection, and health care that require visual image information [6–11]. Computer Vision fusions can present more security system in an IoT platform for smart homes.

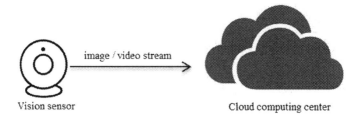

image / video stream

Vision sensor   Cloud computing center

Fig. 1. Cloud-based face recognition system

The local-based face recognition system of Fig. 2, after the vision sensor acquires the image data again, the image data is transmitted to the local computing device through direct connection for comparison and analysis. The advantage is that it will not be disturbed by the network conditions and it will be processed quickly. The disadvantage is that the local processing hardware system based on artificial intelligence technology is expensive and the installation is inconvenient.

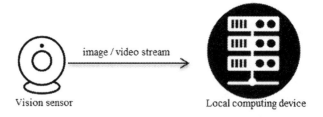

image / video stream

Vision sensor   Local computing device

Fig. 2. Local-based face recognition system

Based on these two recognition systems, this paper proposes a face recognition system based on AI Edge and cloud computing (AE-FRS), which not only has lower network delay time than the traditional cloud-based system, but also lowering the cost and easier to install than local face recognition system.

The following framework of this paper is as follows. Section 2 will describe the problems solved in this paper. Section 3 will introduce the face recognition scheme based on edge AI and cloud computing in detail. Section 4 will prove the effectiveness of the proposed scheme through experiments. Section 5 is the conclusion of this paper. Work with in future.

2   Problem Formations

The purpose of this article is to significantly reduce the response delay of cloud-based face recognition solutions. The response delay in the face recognition system is shown in Formula 1, t_{delay} represents the delay time until the visual sensor obtains the image until the recognition result returns, and the size is determined by the time spent in each step of the recognition process.

t_{delay} is mainly composed of three parts, the first part is the time delay t_{trans} transmitted from the visual sensor to the identification processing center, the second part is the processing center wait time t_{wait} (mainly due to the queue when the processing volume is large), and the third part is Recognition time t_{rec}, the size of which is determined by the algorithm's time complexity and hardware calculation speed.

$$t_{delay} = t_{trans} + t_{wait} + t_{rec} \qquad (1)$$

In Sect. 3, we will describe how to reduce the system's response latency through edge AI. Since the edge AI's capability is sufficient to meet the requirements, and after a real test (see Sect. 4 for details), we will ignore the processing time of the edge AI.

3   AE-FRS

Compared with the old cloud-based face recognition system, AE-FRS will complete a part of the image processing that needs to be processed in the cloud due to the powerful computing power of the edge AI, which will greatly reduce the response delay. At the same time because of the edge AI and the need for complex identification calculations, will not increase the excessive local equipment overhead. We can see from Fig. 3 that compared with cloud-based systems, this system is more than happy local preprocessing. The following will explain in detail the work performed by the preprocessing and how to reduce the response delay of the system.

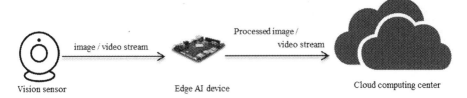

Fig. 3. AE-FRS

As shown in Fig. 4, the preprocessing is mainly divided into the following four steps: (1) background information processing (2) removal of background interference (3) removal of interference repeatedly identified by the same person (4) facial region reduction. Each step is described in detail below.

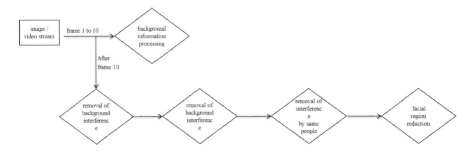

Fig. 4. Pretreatment

Step 1: background information processing, the main purpose is to eliminate the background of the human face interference, such as posters, billboards and other still face images. In real life, the scene that needs to be recognized may have the existence of interfered portrait, which not only brings extra recognition overhead but also takes up the file content to waste network traffic. Because of the calculation ability based on edge AI, this system uses the model based on Uniform Pattern LBP eigenvalue to detect the position of the face in the photo.

After the boot, the system checks a frame of an image every second, and the set of rectangular regions of a face detected in a frame I image is $S^i = \{s_1^i, s_2^i, s_3^i \ldots \ldots s_k^i\}$, s_k^i represents the location of the k-face detected in frame i, $s_k^i = (x_k^i, y_k^i, w_k^i, h_k^i)$. As shown in Fig. 5, x_k^i denotes the distance between the face rectangle image and the left boundary of the k-frame image, y_k^i denotes the distance between the face rectangle image and the boundary on the k-frame image, w_k^i denotes the width of the face rectangle image, and h_k^i denotes the height of the face rectangle image is indicated.

If a face rectangle appears in more than six frames, it is stored in the background interference region set S_{back}. Because the local area of the face in ten frames is rarely fully overlapped, we regard the rectangular area with an overlap ratio of more than 90% as a coincidence, and the other reclosing areas mentioned in this paper are also defined

Fig. 5. Face rectangular region

in the same way. A method of calculating the overlap ratio r of the k face rectangle of frame i and the l face rectangle region of frame j such as formula 2.

$$r = \frac{\left(s_k^i \cap s_l^j\right)}{\left(s_k^i \cup s_l^j\right)} \tag{2}$$

Step 2: remove background interference. After the previous step to determine the background interference S_{back}, the system entered normal working mode. After obtaining a frame of image from the visual sensor, the rectangular region of the face in the current frame is obtained by using the eigenvalue model based on Uniform Pattern LBP. If there is a rectangular region of the face, it should be compared with the rectangular region in the background interference set. Remove overlapping rectangular areas of the face.

Step 3: remove repeated interference from the same person. In the traditional image recognition system, when a continuous frame is recognized, if a person is still in the image, it will cause additional network overhead and recognition overhead for multiple recognition of that person, resulting in the delay of normal face recognition. Therefore, by comparing the face rectangular region set S_{k-1} of the previous frame with the face rectangle region of the frame, the final face region set S_{final}^i of the first frame is obtained by removing the overlapped region.

Step 4: make facial cuts. In face recognition, the traditional cloud system directly pushes the complete image or video stream, in which the redundant background information such as scenery, objects and so on occupying a large amount of image content, resulting in additional network overhead. The cloud recognition center needs information about the face and its vicinity. The final facial region set S_{final}^i obtained by the pre-recording step will be clipped according to the position of the facial region and the cut image will be transmitted to the cloud for processing and recognition. In order to avoid the lack of image information near the face area, we can magnify the rectangular area of the face by a certain multiple (the default 1.2 times) and upload it.

The image processing recognition section of the cloud will be described in a separate article. Because of the edge AI based processing, the number of images uploaded and the size of the image are greatly reduced, thus reducing the t_{trans} and t_{wait}, thus reducing the t_{delay}.

4 Performances and Evaluation

In order to verify the effectiveness of this system, this paper uses rk3288 development platform, webcam, remote server background to build a set of identification system to prove the effectiveness of the system (Fig. 6).

Fig. 6. System hardware equipment

The parameters of system are shown in Table 1.

Table 1. System parameters

	Parameters
Pixel	2048(H) × 1536(V)
Video frame rate	30 fps
Focal length	2.8 mm
Main frequency	Four core A17, main frequency 1.8 Ghz
Memory	2 Ghz
Display card	Mali T760
Uplink bandwidth	500 k/s
Downlink bandwidth	2 M/s
Identification frequency	1 fps

In order to verify the processing speed of edge AI, the images containing 100, 500, 1000, 2000 and 5000 human images were transferred to rk3288 to obtain the time delay from the input image to the final rectangular region S_{final}^i. You can see that it's stable at around 0.3 s (Fig. 7).

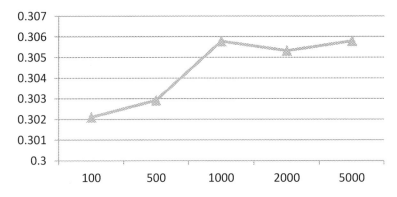

Fig. 7. Processing delay of edge AI

In order to verify the delay comparison between this paper's scheme and the cloud-based face recognition scheme, the rk3288 operation will be applied to the image set containing 100, 500, 1000, 2000, and 5000 portraits respectively, and the time from the image input to the server to return the verification result will be obtained. From the Fig. 8, we can see that the delay of the traditional cloud scheme of blue-folded modern (cyan line) watches has an average value of more than 5 s. With the increase in the number of photos, the delay is significantly increased. The increase in the number of images is 2,000. The cloud center handles the congestion. The purple broken line represents the edge-based AI-based cloud processing system. Its average delay is more than 2 s, and its delay does not increase or decrease significantly, because it eliminates photos that will bring extra recognition costs and reduces the size of the image required for recognition.

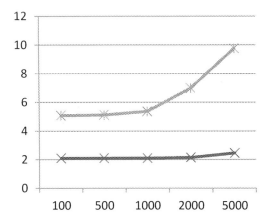

Fig. 8. Compare with traditional cloud-based scheme

5   Conclusions and Future Works

Experiments show that compared with the traditional face recognition cloud system, the face recognition system based on edge AI and cloud computing center proposed in this paper can effectively reduce the delay.

In the future work, we will continue to modify the relevant recognition algorithms in the cloud computing center in order to further reducing the delay.

Acknowledgement. This work is partially supported by the technical projects No. 2016YFB1000803, No. 2017YFB1400604, No. 2017YFB0802703, No. 2012FU125Q09, No. 2015B010131008 and No. JSGG20160331101809920.

References

1. Medina, C.A., Perez, M.R., Trujillo, L.C.: IoT paradigm into the smart city vision: a survey. In: 2017 IEEE International Conference on Internet of Things (iThings) and IEEE Green Computing and Communications (GreenCom) and IEEE Cyber, Physical and Social Computing (CPSCom) and IEEE Smart Data (SmartData), 21–23 June 2017
2. Borgia, E.: The internet of things vision: key features, applications and open issues. Comput. Commun. **54**, 1–31 (2014)
3. Ericsson: More than 50 billion connected devices. Ericsson white paper, pp. 1–12 (2011)
4. Internet of things (IoT) 2013 to 2020 market analysis: Billions of things, trillions of dollars. International Data Corporation, Technical Report (2013)
5. Yigitoglu, E., Mohamed, M., Liu, L., Ludwig, H.: Foggy: a framework for continuous automated IoT application deployment in fog computing. In: 2017 IEEE 6th International Conference on AI and Mobile Services, June 2017
6. Munaro, M., Basso, F., Menegatti, E.: Tracking people within groups with RGB-D data. In: 2012 IEEE/RSJ International Conference on Intelligent Robots and Systems (IROS), pp. 2101–2107, October 2012
7. Cherubini, A., Chaumette, F.: Visual navigation of a mobile robot with laser-based collision avoidance. Int. J. Robot. Res. **32**(2), 189–205 (2013)
8. Ess, A., Leibe, B., Schindler, K., Van Gool, L.: A mobile vision system for robust multi-person tracking. In: 2008 IEEE Conference on Computer Vision and Pattern Recognition, CVPR 2008, pp. 1–8. IEEE (2008)
9. Piatkowska, E., Belbachir, A., Schraml, S., Gelautz, M.: Spatiotemporal multiple persons tracking using dynamic vision sensor. In: 2012 IEEE Computer Society Conference on Computer Vision and Pattern Recognition Workshops (CVPRW), pp. 35–40, June 2012
10. Reverter Valeiras, D., Orchard, G., Ieng, S.H., Benosman, R.B.: Neuromorphic event-based 3D pose estimation. Front. Neurosci. **9**(522) (2015)
11. Ni, Z., Ieng, S.-H., Posch, C., Regnier, S., Benosman, R.: Visual tracking using neuromorphic asynchronous event-based cameras. Neural Comput. **27**(4), 925–953 (2015)
12. Belhumeur, P.N., Hespanha, J.P., Kriegman, D.: Eigenfaces vs. fisherfaces: recognition using class specific linear projection. IEEE Trans. Pattern Anal. Mach. Intell. **19**(7), 711–720 (2007)

A Robust Retail POS System Based on Blockchain and Edge Computing

Bo Hu[1,2], Hongfeng Xie[1], Yutao Ma[3(✉)], Jian Wang[3], and Liang-Jie Zhang[1,2]

[1] Kingdee International Software Co., Ltd., Shenzhen 518057, People's Republic of China
[2] NERC of Enterprise Internet Supporting Software,
Shenzhen 518057, People's Republic of China
[3] Institute of Intelligent Software and Services, School of Computer Science,
Wuhan University, Wuhan 430072, People's Republic of China
ytma@whu.edu.cn

Abstract. New Retail has recently become one of the hottest concepts in the world, particularly in China. Many Internet technologies like Cloud Computing have been employed to address the limitations of the traditional retail industry, and significant progress has been made towards this direction. Despite these achievements, an intractable issue faced by the existing cloud-based retail POS systems is that they cannot provide continuous services when the Internet connections are interrupted. Towards this issue, in this paper, we leverage two new technologies, Blockchain and Edge Computing, to design and develop a new robust retail POS system. More specifically, this type of POS systems deployed in a retail store can use blockchain networking, trustworthiness, and security. We take all cash registers as nodes to build a POS blockchain network and store transaction records in the blockchain network to deal with unexpected network interruptions. Once the Internet connection recovers, a node in the blockchain network will be selected as a POS edge computing server to synchronize data with the POS cloud and resume regular communication between them. The advantages of the robust retail POS system over traditional POS systems include less dependency on the Internet in case of sudden interruptions and little or no hands-on intervention required for changes in our POS system caused by external changes.

Keywords: New retail · POS system · Blockchain · Edge computing

1 Introduction

Recently, *New Retail* has become one of the most popular concepts in the world, particularly in China, and it is considered to be an optimal combination of physical and online retails [1]. Despite a commercial hype to some extent, a few famous Internet companies like Alibaba [2] and Amazon [3] have released their high-level solutions to New Retail, such as mobile payment and self-service supermarket. Even so, there are still many different types of problems to be solved. According to the best practices of the Internet in other industries (e.g., e-Business and e-Government), we believe that traditional retail problems will be tackled by new Internet technologies, business models, and operating

S. Liu et al. (Eds.): EDGE 2018, LNCS 10973, pp. 99–110, 2018.
https://doi.org/10.1007/978-3-319-94340-4_8

methods. Moreover, the Internet will reshape the infrastructure of the traditional retail industry.

As we know, the Retail Point of Sale (POS) System is a critical component of the traditional retail infrastructure. From the perspective of necessity, a retail POS system is also one of the essential IT systems in modern retail stores. Nowadays, an increasing number of retail POS systems begin to transform from a single machine to a cloud terminal. For large retail chains, standard cloud-based retail POS systems can help managers monitor and control their operations more directly and globally. A cloud-based retail POS system uses the "cloud + terminal" mode, in which the management system for orders, inventory, and funds is placed in the cloud (or called POS cloud), while the terminal includes cash registers which can connect to the POS cloud via the Internet or a dedicated network. Generally speaking, this type of cloud-based retail POS systems is efficient enough for most retail chains. Due to the unforeseeable failure of Internet equipment, instability of access to the Internet environment, and other specific factors, it is straightforward to cause an unexpected interruption of the connection to the Internet. As a result, local retail stores fail to sell any products, thus affecting their business operations and customer experience severely.

Developing a robust POS system has always been a matter for software engineers, and setting up a transactional cache locally in a cash register is one of the standard solutions. However, these existing approaches usually result in two issues. On the one hand, although the connection of a retail POS system to the POS cloud is out of service, other systems and terminals continue to work, possibly leading to data conflicts in the data synchronization process after network recovery. On the other hand, during the period of disconnection to the Internet, the security in offline transactions of the retail POS system cannot be guaranteed because the transaction environment is not credible. Inspired by the ideas of Blockchain and Edge Computing, the primary goal of this work is to design and develop a novel retail POS system. This type of retail POS systems can be deployed in a particular area in a retail store, using the mechanisms of blockchain networking, trustworthiness, and security. In particular, to deal with sudden network interruptions, all cash registers of a retail POS system act as nodes to build a POS blockchain network and store the related transaction records in it. Besides, once the access of the retail POS system to the Internet recovers, a node in the blockchain network will be selected as a POS edge computing server to synchronize data with the POS cloud and resume regular communication between them.

The rest of this paper is organized as follows. Section 2 introduces the preliminaries to this study, mainly including the concept, explanation, and applications of Blockchain and Edge Computing. Section 3 presents specific requirements and application scenarios of our work. Section 4 describes the details of blockchain-enabled transactions, including the definition of a POS block, the method of building a POS blockchain network, and the transaction process based on the POS blockchain. Section 5 presents the selection mechanism of a POS edge computing server as well as the communication mechanism between the POS edge computing server and the cloud. Section 6 introduces the development and implementation of the proposed retail POS system by an example. Finally, Sect. 7 concludes the paper.

2   Preliminaries to This Work

2.1   Blockchain

Blockchain, initially Block Chain, is an underlying technology of Bitcoin. It is a decentralized transparent ledger with transaction records—the database that is shared by all network nodes, updated by miners, monitored by everyone, and owned and controlled by no one [4]. As a best practice, it enables Bitcoin [5], a new digital currency, running well to describe how assets are transferred between buyers and sellers. Although blockchain was not first proposed in Satoshi Takemoto's paper, it is increasingly recognized by both the academia and industry and becomes gradually independent of the bitcoin system. In addition to Bitcoin, blockchain, emerged as an independent and promising technology, has been used in many application scenarios, such as food safety traceability and judicial electronic data security.

2.2   Edge Computing

Edge Computing is a new computing paradigm increasingly emerged after Cloud Computing and Internet of Things (IoT). According to the definition of IEEE Report, it refers to "the enabling technologies allowing computation to be performed at the edge of the network, on downstream data on behalf of cloud services and upstream data on behalf of IoT services" [6, 7]. Edge Computing is suitable for the scenarios that data is continuously generated and needs to be processed quickly and timely, but current network bandwidth is not enough to deliver these data to the cloud for processing, such as mobile communications, unmanned driving and so on.

3   Requirements and Application Scenarios

There are two types of popular POS systems in the market, one of which is the local type and the other is cloud-based. The former type of POS systems represents that the entire POS system works inside a retail store, including financial, invoicing and other management software, as well as a cash register. This local POS system does not need to interact with the corresponding systems of other retail stores, and such a system usually does not fail unless its LAN (Local Area Network) is unavailable. However, this type of local POS systems is often limited in the scope of applications, and they are more suitable for small-scale retail companies that own only one store.

For large-scale chain stores, the cloud-based POS system is undoubtedly a preferable choice. First, such a POS system can save the money, time, and labor costs of deploying the system in various retail stores. Second, this type of cloud-based POS systems can monitor and control the operations of all stores distributed in various places. Moreover, it is also beneficial to the cloud-based management and coordination between different stores, such as out-of-stock warnings and out-of-town transfers. However, the disadvantage of the cloud-based POS system is that it is always affected by the Internet environment. Once the network of a store is suddenly interrupted, the operation of the store will undoubtedly be limited to a standstill. To the best of our knowledge, there have been several related attempts before, for example, a transaction is cached to a local cash register and then synchronized to the cloud after the network recovers from a failure. However, due to unsafety and unreliable local environment as well as the instability of data synchronization, the current realizations are prone to cause data loss and accounting errors. In the absence of the Internet, any cash register is considered to be a un-trust machine without the support of the POS cloud because it is accessible to be attacked.

Inspired by the ideas of Blockchain and Edge Computing, we develop a robust retail POS system in which cash registers can continue to work after the connection to the Internet is interrupted. The network topology of this system is different from that of the traditional cloud-based POS system. As shown in Fig. 1, in the traditional cloud-based POS system, any cash register in a retail store is directly connected to the POS cloud and communicates with the POS cloud. In other words, each cash register is a relatively independent device, and there is no interaction between each other. Figure 2 shows the network topology of the new POS system proposed in this paper. The most significant feature of this system architecture is the self-selection of running mode for each cash register when the network of a retail store fails. More specifically, if each cash register cannot connect directly to the POS cloud, it will quickly switch to the off-line mode. They organize together autonomously and automatically to form an internal peer-to-peer network. The POS system then selects a specific node in the peer-to-peer network as a POS edge computing server which communicates with the cloud and transfers data after the access to the Internet is recovered.

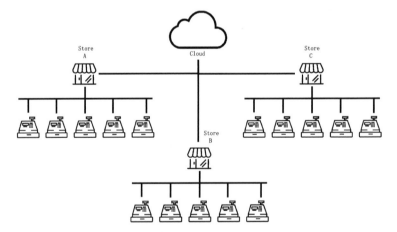

Fig. 1. Traditional cloud-based POS system architecture: every retail store adopts the mode of connecting to the cloud directly through a router and a backbone network.

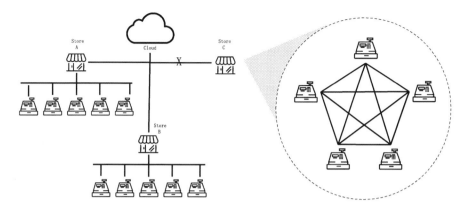

Fig. 2. The network topology of the new POS system. In case of network failure, all cash registers in this retail store do not connect directly to the POS cloud but first form an internal peer-to-peer network. The POS system then selects a specific node in the peer-to-peer network to communicate with the POS cloud and transfer data.

Here, the peer-to-peer network in the retail store is a private blockchain (network). It can be used to build trust and establish a decentralized system that does not require a foundation of mutual trust or relies on a single centralized organization to guarantee the security and traceability of transactions.

Selecting a node as the POS edge computing server is responsible for communicating with the POS cloud and synchronizing transaction information between the local block-chain and the POS cloud, ensuring that our POS system can synchronize all local transaction information to the POS cloud accurately. Whether the network of a retail store is available, the cash registers of the retail store are not affected. Once the network is interrupted or unavailable, the local blockchain does not choose to synchronize data periodically but resumes data synchronization after the network connection to the POS cloud is re-established.

4   Blockchain-Enabled Transactions

4.1   The Definition of a POS Block

A POS block is the basic unit of a POS blockchain, including the information, called the head of the block that will be added to a blockchain, and the details of transactions. In this article, we define the primary data structure of a POS block in Table 1, and the head of a POS block includes:

(1) *Index*: the position of this block in the entire blockchain;
(2) *Timestamp*: the build time of the current block;
(3) *Previous hash*: the hash value of the previous block;
(4) *Proof of Work* (POW): proving the correctness of the work generated by the new block.

Table 1. The primary data structure of a POS block.

Part	Element
Head	Index
	Timestamp
	Previous hash
	Proof of Work
Transaction	Transaction stream ID
	Trading time
	Trading commodity information
	Transaction amount
	Transaction ID
	Transaction hash

Moreover, the elements of a transaction include:

(1) *Transaction stream ID*: a five-tuple composed of cash register identification, system user ID, transaction time, transaction serial number, and random number generating the transaction. This element is used to globally identify the uniqueness of the transaction, as well as to trace the time and location of the transaction and the participants involved in the transaction.

(2) *Trading time*: the specific time of the transaction.

(3) *Trading commodity information*: an array that records the identification information of commodities involved in the transaction, the price of each commodity, the quantity of each commodity, and the actual sales price of each commodity.

(4) *Transaction amount*: the total amount generated in a transaction.

(5) *Transaction ID*: buyer identification.

(6) *Transaction hash*: the hash value of the above transaction information used to ensure that the transaction information is not modified.

4.2   Building a POS Blockchain Network

The trust relationship between nodes is fundamental to building a POS blockchain network. In this sub-section, we will focus on the security networking mechanism of the proposed POS blockchain, which depends mainly on the CA certificate.

Figure 3 depicts the core components of this mechanism and how they work. These core components include:

- **CA Services:** They are used to issue trusted digital certificates to cash registers so that these cash registers can form a blockchain.
- **POS Certification:** This certification contains the POS machine's public key, POS machine information, and digital summary information.

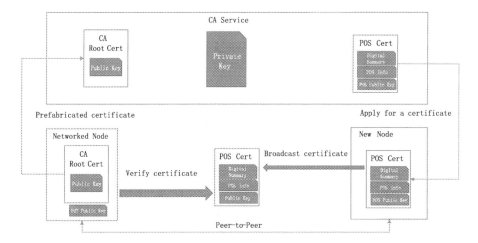

Fig. 3. Core components of the security networking mechanism of the proposed POS blockchain and how they work with each other.

When a new node is ready to join the blockchain network, the new node first initiates a broadcast sending the certificate. After the networked nodes have received the certificate, they would like to let the new node join the blockchain network after the certificate has been verified to be true.

4.3 POS Blockchain-Based Transactions

Figure 4 shows the whole transaction process of the proposed POS blockchain, including the following four steps.

Step 1: Generate transactions and broadcast. In the POS blockchain network, any node can generate transactions, and each transaction generated by any node will be transferred to other nodes in a manner of broadcasting. Each node needs to maintain a blockchain and can accept transactions generated by all nodes and write these transactions into a new block. Typically, each block may have hundreds or thousands of transactions.

Step 2: Verify transactions and reach a consensus. Although each node can receive transactions and write them into new blocks, the determination of a node which owns the most realistic transactions requires a consensus among all the nodes in the network. In our method, the POW is very simple. Each node which records a ledger will obtain the right of verification. It can broadcast the hash information of all transactions to the entire network and compare the information with other nodes.

Step 3: Broadcast the new block. The node that can first complete the POW is recognized to own the certified new block, and it will broadcast its block to other nodes in the blockchain network.

Step 4: Add the new block to the blockchain. Other nodes will confirm whether the transaction contained in this block is valid. After confirming that the transaction has not been duplicated and has a sign of validity, a node can accept the block. At this time,

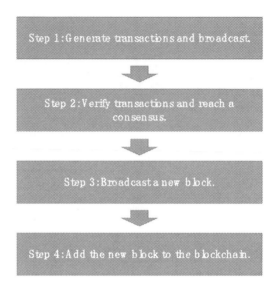

Fig. 4. The whole transaction process of the POS blockchain.

the block is officially linked to the blockchain, and the data of the block can no longer be modified. Once all nodes have accepted the block, other blocks which did not finish the POW work before become invalid, and each node will re-establish a block and continue the next POW calculation.

5   Data Synchronization Based on Edge Computing

When the network resumes work, the new retail POS system we develop will restore the online mode. Before this mode is turned on, the transactions generated in the offline mode and recorded in the POS blockchain must be synchronized to the POS cloud. The synchronization process requires a node selected from the POS blockchain network to be responsible for the work of data synchronization. Here, the selected node is called a POS edge computing server.

The selection of a POS edge computing server is currently straightforward. The POS blockchain network is a peer-to-peer network, in which each node has complete POS blockchain information as well as all the transaction data. Theoretically, any node in the POS blockchain network can be used as a POS edge computing server to synchronize data with the POS cloud. In our system, we choose the node which first completes the POW before the end of the offline mode as the edge computing server. When it finishes broadcasting new blocks to other nodes, it starts to synchronize data with the POS cloud as quickly as possible.

6   Development and Implementation

We implemented the retail POS system in JDY.com. JDY.com is the largest management software and cloud service in China, provided by Kingdee. In particular, it provides new retail solutions such as POS System for medium, small- and micro-sized enterprises. Before this, JDY.com provided a variety of traditional POS system solutions for retailers with cash registers based on the Android and iOS platforms. As stated at the beginning of the paper, the traditional cloud-based POS system is designed based on the Internet. Once the access to the Internet is unavailable, the cash register equipment cannot transfer data to the cloud promptly, possibly leading to financial losses of retail stores.

Here, we improved these traditional POS systems according to the solution mentioned in this paper. For each cash register, we provide a packaged SDK (Software Development Kit) integration into its terminal system software. Any cash register does not connect directly to the POS cloud when it starts. The retail POS system obtains other similar devices in the same local area network by broadcasting, shaping a peer-to-peer network through two-way links. Then, a POS blockchain comes into being. Of course, we also made some modifications in the cloud to be able to synchronize transaction data in the local blockchain.

Figures 5 and 6 show how cash registers work after the retail POS system updates. Figure 5 is an overview screenshot from the POS cloud. It depicts a business case with a total of three retail stores in a particular area in Shenzhen city. Each point on the map represents a retail store, and the different colors of the points represent different network states of the three retail stores. Among the three retail stores, the blue dot indicates that the retail store network is healthy, and the red dot indicates that the network is abnormal. In other words, all the cash registers in the three retail stores represented by the red dot cannot connect to the POS cloud.

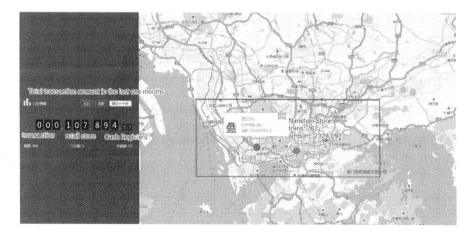

Fig. 5. A business case with a total of three retail stores in a specific area in Shenzhen. More specifically, each point on the map represents a retail store, and the different colors of the points represent different network states of the retail stores. Note that the blue dot indicates that the retail store network is healthy and the red dot indicates that the network is abnormal.

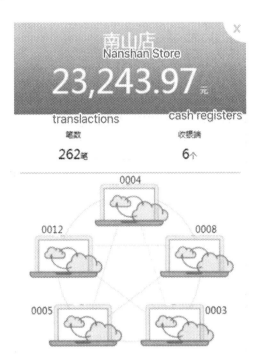

Fig. 6. Five cash registers have successfully formed a POS blockchain after the network of the retail store was unavailable.

Figure 6 depicts a typical cash-collection scenario when an individual retail store is abnormal on the Internet from the viewpoint of a cash register. From this figure, we can see that there are six cash registers in this retail store with an abnormal Internet state. Among all the cash registers, five cash registers have successfully constituted a POS blockchain after the network was interrupted. Moreover, at this time, the retail store's transaction is continued from the time of the disconnection to the time of screenshot. A total of 262 transactions were successfully conducted, and the transaction amount exceeded 23,000 RMB.

Figures 7 and 8 show a comparison of the changes in the synchronization of specific transaction data between different nodes in the blockchain. Figure 7 shows the screen-shot of the cash register under discussion before the transaction was synchronized. At this time, there was a total of 2 transactions with a transaction value of 228 RMB. Figure 8 displays the result of sales data of other cash registers synchronizing to the cash register via the POS blockchain. The transaction amount is a little more than that shown in Fig. 7, for a total of 3 transactions with a transaction value of 248 RMB.

Fig. 7. The screenshots of the cash register in question before the transaction was synchronized.

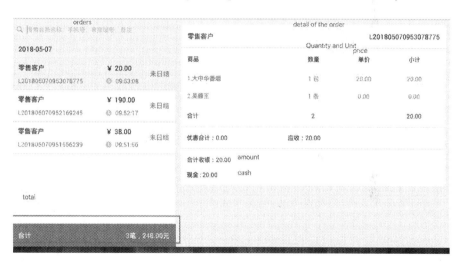

Fig. 8. The result of other cash registers' sales data synchronizing to this cash register via the POS blockchain.

7   Conclusion

The article is an application-typed paper. In this paper, we propose and develop a novel robust POS system based on the technologies of Blockchain and Edge Computing for retail chains, which can be used in "weak" Internet environments. A "weak" Internet environment implies that when the Internet connection of a retail store is suddenly interrupted, cash registers in this store will turn on the off-line mode to continue work.

In this off-line mode, each cash register can form a POS blockchain network, in which each node can trade and maintain blocks, and the transaction of all nodes is recorded by the blockchain to ensure that the transaction is complete and reliable. When the access to the Internet becomes available, these cash registers will be switched to the online mode. A node with a full block in the POS blockchain network will be selected as a POS edge computing server to communicate with the POS cloud. The selected POS edge computing server synchronizes these off-line transactions to the POS cloud, and then the whole retail POS system can be restored to regular use. The advantages of the robust retail POS system compared with the traditional POS systems include two aspects. On the one hand, our POS system does not always rely on the Internet if the Internet access is suddenly interrupted, thus making retail stores less affected by the network failure. On the other hand, changes in the POS system caused by external changes in the Internet are automated and do not require manual intervention.

Acknowledgement. This application research was supported by the National Key Research and Development Program of China (Nos. 2017YFB1400604 and 2016YFB1000803), National Science Foundation of China (Nos. 61672387 and 61702378), and the Wuhan Yellow Crane Talents Program for Modern Services Industry.

References

1. Gallino, S., Moreno, A.: Integration of online and offline channels in retail: the impact of sharing reliable inventory availability information. Manage. Sci. **60**(6), 1434–1451 (2014)
2. Glowik, M.: 4.1 case study: Alibaba group. In: Global Strategy in the Service Industries: Dynamics, Analysis, Growth, vol. 96 (2017)
3. Kowalkiewicz, M., Rosemann, M., Dootson, P.: Retail 5.0: Check Out the Future (2017)
4. Swan, M.: Blockchain: Blueprint for a New Economy. O'Reilly Media, Inc (2015)
5. Nakamoto, S.: Bitcoin: A Peer-To-Peer Electronic Cash System, October 2008 (2017). http://www.bitcoin.org/bitcoin.Pdf
6. Shi, W., Cao, J., Zhang, Q., et al.: Edge computing: vision and challenges. IEEE Internet Things J. **3**(5), 637–646 (2016)
7. Sharma, P.K., Chen, M.-Y., Park, J.H.: A software defined fog node based distributed blockchain cloud architecture for IoT. IEEE Access **6**, 115–124 (2018)

A Privacy Risk Aware Service Selection Approach for Service Composition

Mingdong Tang[1,2(✉)], Jianguo Xie[1], and Sumeng Zeng[2]

[1] School of Information Science and Technology,
Guangdong University of Foreign Studies, Guangzhou 510006, China
mdtang@126.com
[2] School of Computer Science and Engineering,
Hunan University of Science and Technology, Xiangtan 411201, China

Abstract. Service composition has been widely used to fulfill a complex task when a single service cannot meet its functional requirement. In dynamic service composition, selecting appropriate services from all service candidates is a critical issue. Most previous work focused on service selection based on the services' functionalities and quality, so that the user's requirements can be well satisfied. However, more and more service users are concerned about their privacy in the Internet era. Therefore, it is increasingly important for selecting services that preserves the privacy of service users. To address the shortcomings of previous work, this paper proposes a privacy risk aware service selection approach for service composition. Based on the user's privacy preservation requirement, the approach is intended to obtain a service composition that minimize the user's privacy risk. To do this, we use the service dependency graph to model the relationships between services and define the above service composition problem as searching an optimal path with the least privacy risk on the graph. The privacy risk of an individual service to the user is computed by integrating the user's personal privacy preservation requirement, the service's privacy policy and the service's reputation. Examples and empirical evaluations validated the proposed approach in reducing the privacy risk of service users.

Keywords: Service composition · Service selection · Privacy preservation
Reputation · Service network

1 Introduction

The Internet has become a platform for provision and consumption of various services such as Web services, cloud services and mobile services. With the abundant services, service composition has been widely accepted as a promising approach for new application creation. In general, service composition approaches can be divided into two categories: static composition and dynamic composition [1]. Static service composition refers to a class of approaches that service users have to select and compose services manually according to their requirements. Therefore, the service composition occurs in the design stage. Dynamic service composition refers to a class of approaches

© Springer International Publishing AG, part of Springer Nature 2018
S. Liu et al. (Eds.): EDGE 2018, LNCS 10973, pp. 111–123, 2018.
https://doi.org/10.1007/978-3-319-94340-4_9

that service users only need to define tasks with machine readable languages and forward them to an execution engine, which in turn will automatically select appropriate services and compose them according to the tasks' description. Actually, dynamic service composition is much more challenging than static service composition, and thus has gained increasing attention in the past decade. To attack this issue, dozens of dynamic service composition approaches have been proposed [2, 3]. The critical issue is how to select suitable services so that the automatically generated service composition can satisfy both functional and quality requirements of the task defined by the user. The quality requirements on services are typically referred to as a group of criteria like availability, reliability, latency, cost, reputation, etc.

Previous service selection and composition approaches seldom took the user's privacy concern into consideration, which, however, has become one of the most important issues in the Internet era [4]. As a matter of fact, many services on the Internet require users to provide personal information, such as name, telephone number, credit card number, email and location, to enhance its service quality. For example, an online meal ordering and delivery service may ask a user to provide his/her exact location and phone number, so that it can recommend the nearest restaurants to the user and deliver the food successfully as soon as possible. Once the private information of a user was obtained by the service provider, the service provider may abuse it or leak it out, thus making the user's privacy at risk. The user privacy risk is likely to be even exaggerated, when service composition is concerned. That is, when a user is invoking a service composition which comprises several services, his/her private information may have to be repeatedly exposed to the multiple services. As a result, the user privacy risk is multiplicated.

To reduce the privacy risk faced by users in service composition, this paper proposes a privacy preservation-oriented service selection approach for service composition. Based on the service graph [5] or service network [6] model, we assume that all services have been connected as a network according to their dependency relations. Therefore, the service composition problem can be defined as a subgraph or path search problem on the graph, as long as satisfying the user's functional and non-functional requirements. For simplicity, we only consider the path search problem in this paper. In this regard, the proposed approach aims at searching an optimal path with the least privacy risk on the service network. The privacy risk of an individual service to the user is assessed by integrating the user's personal privacy preservation requirement, the service's privacy policy and the service's reputation. Examples and empirical evaluations validated the effectiveness and efficiency of the proposed approach.

The rest of this paper is organized as follows. Section 2 presents some definitions and formalizes the research problem. Section 3 describes the proposed service selection and composition approach. Section 4 uses an example to illustrate the steps of the proposed approach. Section 5 evaluates the time performance of the proposed approach. Section 6 surveys related work. Finally, Sect. 7 concludes this paper with future work.

2 Definitions

In this section, we firstly define some important concepts used in our approach, such as service network, user privacy preference, service privacy policy and service reputation. Then, we formulate the service composition and service selection problem.

2.1 Service Network

Based on the models of Service Dependency Graph (SDG) [5] and Service Network [6], we define a service network as a directed graph showing all possible interactions and dataflow relationships among the services in a given service set. In other words, all possible input and output relationships of the services are revealed in a service network. We can process a user's service request against the service network to determine if a structure of services can be found to meet the service request. An example of service network is given in Fig. 1. This service network consists of four services: *AirTicket Booking*, *Hotel Booking* 1, *Hotel Booking* 2, and *Scenic Spot Recommendation*. The text besides each service represents the input data required by it. Directed edges represent the data flows between services, and the text on the edges represents the data output by a service to another. For example, the *AirTicket Booking* service needs input data like customer name, customer id, destination, departure city, departure time, phone number, etc., and would output data to a hotel booking service like arrival time and destination. Formally, we define service network as follows:

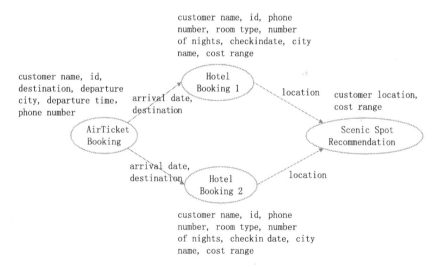

Fig. 1. An example of service network

Definition 1 (Service Network): A service network can be defined using a directed graph $G = (V, E, I, O)$, where V is the set of the services, E is the set of edges that represent the data flows among services, I represents the set of input data needed by services and O represents the set of output data produced by services.

2.2 User Privacy Preference

The typical privacy data concerned by a service user may include name, id, phone number, birthdate, income, email, address and so on. Different users could have different privacy preference, in other words, they are likely to have different sensitiveness to different privacy data items. For example, some service users may consider name more sensitive than phone number, while some other users may not. The following definitions are used to formally describe privacy data and user privacy preference:

Definition 2 (Privacy Data): The privacy data concerned by users can be denoted by the set $I = \{I_1, I_2, ..., I_m\}$, where I_j ($1 \leq j \leq m$) represents a privacy data item.

Definition 3 (Privacy Sensitiveness): Privacy sensitiveness can be described using a partially ordered set $P = (PC, \leq)$, where PC denotes the set of privacy sensitiveness levels, which can be expressed using linguistic terms, i.e., {*very low, low, medium, high, very high*}. The operator $\leq$ is a partial order relation based on PC, so that we have *very low* $\leq$ *low* $\leq$ *medium* $\leq$ *high* $\leq$ *very high*.

Definition 4 (Privacy Preference): A user's privacy preference can be denoted by $F = \{(i, p) \mid i \in I, p \in PC\}$, where i is a privacy data item concerned by the user, and p represents a privacy sensitiveness level.

2.3 Service Reputation and Privacy Policy

In reality, a service user usually depends heavily on the reputation and privacy policy of a service when assessing its risk to his/her privacy. Generally, the higher is the service's reputation, the less risk the user believes that the service will bring to his/her privacy. Therefore, this work takes reputation of service into consideration. The privacy policy of a service usually specifies what privacy data the service will collect from a user. A privacy policy may be very complicated in practice, while this work simplifies it by only considering its privacy data requirement. In the following, we formally define the reputation and privacy policy of a service.

Definition 5 (Service Reputation): Service reputation can be described using a partially ordered set $R = (RC, \leq)$, where RC denotes the set of reputation levels, i.e., {*very low, low, medium, high, very high*}. The operator $\leq$ is a partial order relation based on RC, so that we have *very low* $\leq$ *low* $\leq$ *medium* $\leq$ *high* $\leq$ *very high*.

Definition 6 (Privacy Policy): The privacy policy of a service (s) for users can be defined as a subset of privacy data items $I(s) = \{I_{s,1}, I_{s,2}, ..., I_{s,k}\}$, where $I_{s,j}$ ($1 \leq j \leq k$) represents a privacy data item required by the service. In this work, we assume that the privacy data required by a service is a part of the input data of the service. For example, in Fig. 1, the *AirTicket Booking service*'s input data includes customer name, customer id, destination, departure city, departure time and phone number, among which the customer's name, id and phone number could be claimed as privacy data items in the service's privacy policy.

2.4 Privacy Risk

In the following, we formally define the privacy risk of a data item, a service and a service composition.

Definition 7 (Privacy Risk of a Data Item): There are usually multiple privacy-sensitive data items concerned by a service user. Different privacy data items are likely to have different sensitiveness to the user, and thus have different risk degrees. The risk of an individual privacy data item (i) to a user raised by a service (s) is denoted by $PR_{s,i}$, in this paper. For instance, if a user is very sensitive to his/her address, the privacy risk his/her address should be very high when requesting a service that requires his/her address information. Assessment of the risk of an individual privacy data item depends on the user's sensitiveness on the data item and the service's reputation (more details will be discussed in Sect. 3).

Definition 8 (Privacy Risk of a Service): The privacy risk of a service (s) to a user is calculated based on the privacy risks of all privacy data items supplied by the user to the service. For instance, suppose that a service requires a user to provide privacy-sensitive data such as name, phone number and address. The privacy risk of the service to the user is an aggregation of the privacy risks of individual data items like $PR_{s,name}$, $PR_{s,phone}$, and $PR_{s,address}$.

Definition 9 (Privacy Risk of a Service Composition): The privacy risk of a service composition is calculated based on the privacy risks of all services in the service composition. For instance, suppose there is a service composition (c), which is composed of services s and t. The privacy risk of the service to the user is an aggregation of the individual privacy risks $PR(s)$ and $PR(t)$.

2.5 Privacy Risk Aware Service Selection for Composition

The research problem is defined as: Given a service network consisting of a set of services and a set of dependency relations among them, how to select the optimal path from the network to construct a service composition that not only meets the user's requirements but also has the least privacy risk to the user? Let's take the example in Fig. 1 to illustrate this research problem. Suppose there are two paths of services that satisfy the user's functional requirements, e.g., *AirTicket Booking service -> Hotel Booking service* 1 *-> Scenic Spot Recommendation service* and *AirTicket Booking service -> Hotel Booking service* 2 *-> Scenic Spot Recommendation service*. The two service compositions may have different privacy risks to a user due to that their corresponding component services' reputation and privacy policies are different. It is preferred to select the service path with the less privacy risk. To do this, it is vital to evaluate the privacy risk of each service in the service network that may be needed in service composition, as well as the privacy risk of each path in the service network that satisfies the user's functional requirements, so that optimal service path can be finally identified.

3 The Approach

In this section, we firstly introduce how to compute the risk degree of an individual privacy data item to the user based on the user's privacy preference and the service's reputation. Then, we discuss how to assess the privacy risk degree of a service to the user, which is based on aggregation of the calculated privacy risk degrees of the privacy data items needed by the service. Afterwards, we present an algorithm for optimal service composition selection in a service network, so that the service composition with the least privacy risks would be found for the user.

3.1 Assessment of the Risk Degree of an Individual Privacy Data Item

As defined in Definition 3, sensitiveness of privacy data items can be expressed as the following five levels: *very low*, *low*, *medium*, *high*, *very high*. The reputation of a service is also key to the privacy risk assessment for a user, since it is generally believed that a service with higher reputation would be more trustworthy in preserving the user's privacy. The reputation of a service can also be expressed using five linguistic terms: *very low*, *low*, *medium*, *high*, *very high*, as stated in Definition 5.

Taking the user's privacy preference and the service's reputation into consideration, a set of heuristic rules can be developed to infer the risk of a privacy data item posed by a service to the user, and they are summarized in Fig. 2. Actually, the twenty-five heuristic rules are extended from the general heuristic rules as follows:

1. If the privacy data item is highly sensitive to the user and the reputation of the service is low, the privacy risk is probably high to the user;
2. If the privacy data item is lowly sensitive to the user and the reputation of the service is high, the privacy risk is probably low to the user;
3. If the privacy data item is lowly sensitive to the user and the reputation of the service is low, or the privacy data item is highly sensitive to the user and the reputation of the service is high, the privacy risk is at a medium level.

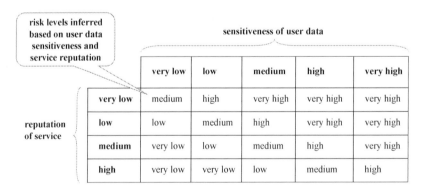

Fig. 2. Inferring the privacy risk levels based on the users' privacy sensitiveness and the service's reputation.

Since both the user privacy sensitiveness and the service reputation have five linguistic terms, the privacy risk degrees can also be expressed using five values: *very low, low, medium, high, very high.*

3.2   Assessment of the Risk Degree of a Single Service

A service usually has a privacy policy for users, which specifies what privacy data items will be collected from a user. Services provided by different vendors are likely to have different privacy policies, i.e., different privacy data requirements, thus raising different risks to a user. To assess the risk degree of a service to a user, it is a necessity to leverage all privacy data items required by the service from the user. In the following, we introduce an aggregate operator to do this. Since the risk degree of each privacy data item is valued in linguistic terms, we firstly transform their values to real numbers. This work uses the centroid method (CM) [7] for defuzzifying linguistic term-based values. The CM, also known as either the center of gravity (CoG) or center of area (CoA) method, is the most commonly used defuzzification technique. This technique provides a crisp value based on the CoG of the fuzzy set. It also determines the best point for dividing the fuzzy set into exactly two masses. Because linguistic terms can be decomposed in a triangular shape, the CM becomes a suitable approach for defuzzifying the linguistic privacy risk terms. For a triangular fuzzy number $F = (\mu, \lambda, \rho)$, its real number value (ω) can be calculated as:

$$\omega = \lambda + \frac{(\mu - \lambda) + (\rho - \lambda)}{3} \tag{1}$$

In this work, five linguistic terms are decomposed into triangular fuzzy numbers using the triangular fuzzy set shown in Fig. 3. These linguistic terms, their fuzzy numbers and corresponding real number values are presented in Table 1.

If I_i and I_j are two privacy data items required by a service, and their assessed privacy risk values are PR_i and PR_j respectively, their privacy risk values can be aggregated as follows:

$$PR_i \wedge PR_j = PR_i + PR_j \tag{2}$$

where $\wedge$ is the aggregate operator. From this equation, we can see more privacy data items provided by a user should cause a higher risk degree to the user.

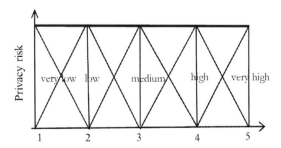

Fig. 3. Triangular membership functions for the five linguistic terms of privacy risk

Table 1. The five linguistic terms, their fuzzy numbers, and corresponding real number values

Linguistic terms	Fuzzy numbers	Real number value
Very high	(4, 5, 5)	4.67
High	(3, 4, 5)	4.00
Medium	(2, 3, 4)	3.00
Low	(1, 2, 3)	2.00
Very low	(1, 1, 2)	1.33

Table 2. The proposed algorithm for finding the optimal path in a service network

---

Algorithm Description

Input: A set of services V, and its service network $G=(V,E)$, privacy preference of the user, privacy policies of services, reputation of services;

Output: The optimal path of services and its overall privacy risk;

S: The subset of services whose distances have been resolved;

$D[]$: Distances of all services to the source;

Do initialization: $S=\{\}$, $D[]=\infty$, $Path[]=s$; //s is the source

$D[s]=0$;

While ($|S| < |V|$)

    Find the service i in $V-S$ so that $D[i]$ is minimal in D;

    For all service j ($i->j\in E$ and $j\in V-S$)

        Calculate the privacy risk value of j (denoted by $PR(j)$);

        If ($D[j] > D[i]+PR(j)$)

            $D[j] = D[i]+PR(j)$;

            $Path[j] \leftarrow Path[i] + j$;

        End If

        $S = S + \{j\}$;

    End For

End While

Output $D[]$ and $Path[]$;

3.3   Optimal Service Composition Finding with the Least Privacy Risk

Similar to previous work [3], this work transforms the dynamic service composition problem to optimal path finding in a service network. Figure 4 is an example showing how to find the optimal path in a service network, where vertices represent services and edges represent dependency relations. The notation besides a vertex represents its assessed privacy risk value. We adapt the Dijkstra algorithm to address this issue, as shown in Table 2. Please note that, the length of a path $s \rightarrow t$ is represented by the

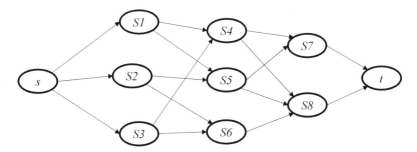

Fig. 4. An example of optimal path finding in a service network based on privacy risks

summation of risk values of all services in the path, and the distance from t to s is defined as the minimal length among all directed paths connecting s with t. Since the best Dijkstra algorithm implementation has time complexity of $O(n\log n + m)$, our proposed algorithm can also be implemented with the same time complexity.

4   Illustrative Example

This section presents an example to illustrate our approach. Suppose that a user wants to arrange a travel by requesting services from a tourism website. The tourism web site responds to the user's request via combining the three kinds of services: air ticket booking, hotel booking, and scenic spot recommendation. Suppose there are three air ticket booking services (i.e., S_1, S_2 and S_3), three hotel booking services (i.e., S_4, S_5 and S_6), and two scenic spot recommendation services (i.e., S_7 and S_8) for selection. Table 3 shows the privacy data items and the user's preference on them. Table 4 shows the privacy requirements and reputation of the above services. The reputation values are crisp values calculated using the defuzzification method presented in Sect. 3.2. Figure 5 shows the dependency relations between the above services. The privacy requirements and reputation values of services are also shown in Fig. 5.

Table 3. Privacy data items and the user's preference on them

	Name (I_1)	Address (I_2)	ID (I_3)	Email (I_4)	#Phone (I_5)	#Credit card (I_6)	#Alipay account (I_7)
Sensitiveness	0.5	0.6	0.3	0.6	0.8	0.7	0.6

Table 5 presents the privacy risk values of different services to the user, which are calculated using Formula 2. For instance, Service 4 (S_4) has the greatest privacy risk value (i.e., 2.4) while Service 1 (S_1) has the smallest privacy risk value (i.e., 1.4). Figure 6 shows the example service network after privacy risk calculation for services. By employing our optimal path searching algorithm, we can obtain the optimal path s -> S_1 > S_5 -> S_7 -> t, which represents the best service composition with the least privacy risk.

Table 4. Privacy requirements and reputation of services

Services	Privacy requirements	Reputation
S_1	I_1, I_2, I_4	0.70
S_2	I_2, I_5, I_6	0.60
S_3	I_1, I_2, I_7	0.80
S_4	I_2, I_3, I_5, I_6	0.65
S_5	I_1, I_3, I_6	0.70
S_6	I_4, I_5, I_7	0.56
S_7	I_3, I_5, I_6	0.60
S_8	I_1, I_3, I_5, I_7	0.63

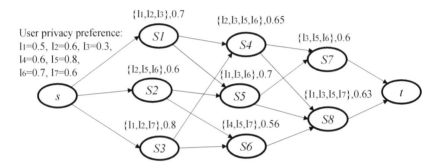

Fig. 5. An example service network with service dependency relations, privacy requirements and reputation values

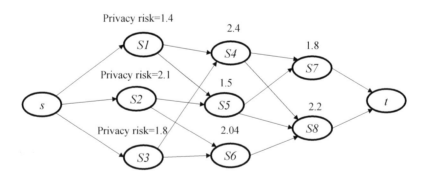

Fig. 6. The example service network after privacy risk calculation for services

Table 5. Privacy risk values of different services to the user

	S_1	S_2	S_3	S_4	S_5	S_6	S_7	S_8
Values	1.40	2.10	1.80	2.40	1.50	2.04	1.80	2.20

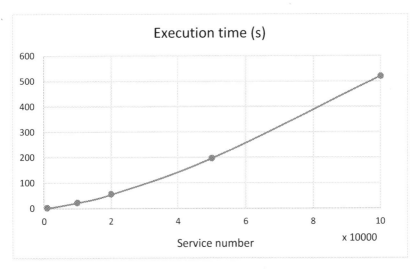

Fig. 7. Time performance

5 Performance Evaluation

This experiment evaluates the time performance of the proposed approach and its scalability with the service number. We use a simulated service network, whose service number is varied from 1 k, 10 k, 20 k, 50 k to 100 k. The experiment program was developed using Java. Figure 7 shows the execution time of the proposed approach versus the number of services. For instance, when the service number is 1 k, the execution time is about 1 s. We can see that the execution time increases slowly with respect to the number of services, which indicates that our proposed approach has a good scalability with the increase of the service number.

6 Related Work

Preserving the user's privacy when requesting services on the Internet has become a requisite and many studies has been conducted on this topic. Most privacy preservation techniques are based on anonymization [8, 9] or encryption [10]. Their basic ideas are to anonymize or encrypt some key values of the user data, so that for each user contained in the data it cannot be identified. The anonymization or encryption techniques can prevent the user's privacy being exposed in data release to some extent. However, they assume that the service provider is trustworthy and will always use the users' data properly, which is unrealistic. Moreover, data leakage or violation may occur inevitably because decryption and anti-anonymization techniques can be applied by malicious users or organizations. Therefore, to reduce the privacy risk or loss of users in service request, policy-based privacy preservation approaches have been proposed for service selection [11]. They allowed a service provider defining privacy requirements using policies and did matchmaking between the user's privacy preference and the service's privacy requirements [12–14] or between two services' privacy requirements for service composition purpose [15–18]. Our previous work [19] proposed a service ranking approach based on privacy risk evaluation, which allows a user specifying his/her privacy preference and a service provider specifying its privacy data requirements with linguistic terms. This work extended our previous work for service composition. We integrate privacy risk computation and a service network model to find a service composition with the least privacy risk.

7 Conclusions

This paper presented a privacy risk aware service selection approach for service composition. The approach assessed a service's risk degree to a user's privacy based on its reputation, privacy policy and the user's privacy preference. To find the best service composition with the least privacy risk, the approach employed a service network model incorporating the dependency relations between services, based on which an optimal path search algorithm for service composition was proposed. Examples and experiments demonstrated that the proposed approach is effective and can perform efficiently. The future work will conduct more evaluations to validate the proposed approach. Moreover, we will take quality of service into consideration, and employ the multi-objective optimization theory to optimize the tradeoff between privacy preservation and quality of service in service selection and composition.

Acknowledgments. The work is supported by the National Natural Science Foundation of China under Grant No. 61572186.

References

1. Lemos, A.L., Daniel, F., Benatallah, B.: Web service composition: a survey of techniques and tools. ACM Comput. Surv. **48**(3), 33:1–33:41 (2016)
2. Yu, T., Zhang, Y., Lin, K.-J.: Efficient algorithms for Web services selection with end-to-end QoS constraints. ACM Trans. Web **1**(1), 6 (2007)
3. Jiang, W., Wu, T., Hu, S., Liu, Z.: QoS-aware automatic service composition: a graph view. J. Comput. Sci. Technol. **26**(5), 837–853 (2011)
4. Featherman, M.S., Miyazaki, A.D., Sprott, D.E.: Reducing online privacy risk to facilitate e-service adoption: the influence of perceived ease of use and corporate credibility. J. Serv. Mark. **24**(3), 219–229 (2010)
5. Gu, Z., Li, J., Xu, B.: Automatic service composition based on enhanced service dependency graph. In: 2008 IEEE International Conference on Web Services (ICWS), pp. 246–253. IEEE Press (2008)
6. Wang, Z., Xu, F., Xu, X.: Service network planning method for mass personalized functional requirements. J. Softw. **25**(6), 1180–1195 (2014)
7. Opricovic, S., Tzeng, G.H.: Defuzzification within a multicriteria decision model. Int. J. Uncertain. Fuzziness Knowl.-Based Syst. **11**(05), 635–652 (2003)
8. Sweeney, L.: k-anonymity: a model for protecting privacy. Int. J. Uncertain. Fuzziness Knowl.-Based Syst. **10**(05), 557–570 (2002)

9. Ammar, N., Malik, Z., Medjahed, B., Alodib, M.: K-anonymity based approach for privacy-preserving web service selection. In: 2015 IEEE International Conference on Web Services (ICWS), pp. 281–288. IEEE Press (2015)
10. Li, X., Jung, T.: Search me if you can: privacy-preserving location query service. In: 2013 IEEE International Conference on Computer Communications (INFOCOM), pp. 2760–2768. IEEE Press (2013)
11. Lin, L., Liu, T., Hu, J., Ni, J.: PQsel: combining privacy with quality of service in cloud service selection. Int. J. Big Data Intell. 3(3), 202–214 (2016)
12. Kapitsaki, G.M.: Reflecting user privacy preferences in context-aware web services. In: 2013 IEEE International Conference on Web Services (ICWS), pp. 123–130. IEEE Press (2013)
13. Squicciarini, A., Carminati, B., Karumanchi, S.: A privacy-preserving approach for web service selection and provisioning. In: 2011 IEEE International Conference on Web Services (ICWS), pp. 33–40. IEEE Press (2011)
14. Lin, L., Liu, T., Hu, J., Zhang, J.: A privacy-aware cloud service selection method toward data life-cycle. In: 20th IEEE International Conference on Parallel and Distributed Systems (ICPADS), pp. 752–759. IEEE Press (2014)
15. Costante, E., Paci, F., Zannone, N.: Privacy-aware web service composition and ranking. In: 2013 IEEE 20th International Conference on Web Services (ICWS), pp. 131–138. IEEE Press (2013)
16. Carminati, B., Ferrari, E., Tran, N.H.: A privacy-preserving framework for constrained choreographed service composition. In: 2015 IEEE International Conference on Web Services (ICWS), pp. 297–304. IEEE Press (2015)
17. Squicciarini, A.C., Carminati, B., Karumanchi, S.: Privacy aware service selection of composite web services. In: 2013 IEEE International Conference on Collaborative Computing: Networking, Applications and Worksharing (Collaboratecom), pp. 260–268. IEEE Press (2013)
18. Tbahriti, S.-E., Ghedira, C., Medjahed, B., Mrissa, M.: Privacy-enhanced Web service composition. IEEE Trans. Serv. Comput. 7(2), 210–222 (2014)
19. Tang, M., Zeng, S., Liu, J., Cao, B.: Service selection based on user privacy risk evaluation. In: Wang, G., Atiquzzaman, M., Yan, Z., Choo, K.-K.R. (eds.) SpaCCS 2017. LNCS, vol. 10656, pp. 308–320. Springer, Cham (2017). https://doi.org/10.1007/978-3-319-72389-1_25

Short Paper Track

A Chinese Text Correction and Intention Identification Method for Speech Interactive Context

Jin Che[1($\boxtimes$)], Huan Chen[1,2], Jing Zeng[1,2,3], and Liang-Jie Zhang[1,2]

[1] Kingdee Research, Kingdee International Software Group Company Limited,
Shenzhen, China
18682213320@163.com
[2] National Engineering Research Center for Supporting Software of Enterprise
Internet Services, Shenzhen, China
[3] Research Institute of Web Information, Tsinghua University, Beijing, China

Abstract. ASR (Automatic Speech Recognition) is an important technology in man-machine interaction. Due to the complexity of natural language, the interference of environment and other factors, the recognition accuracy has low accuracy. This paper analyzes the use cases of speech recognition errors and proposes a text correction and intent recognition method based on the phonation principle and language characteristics peculiar to Chinese, and proposes an improved edit distance method to better calculate the text distance. Through a large number of experiments, this method can improves 22.9% accuracy of text recognition in ASR system.

Keywords: Text correction · Intention identification · ASR

1 Introduction

According to Statista's estimate, the global smart home market will reach 79.3 billion U.S. dollars in 2021. ABI Research's predictions are more optimistic. It is predicted that the global smart home market will reach 70 billion U.S. dollars in 2018 and 100 billion U.S. dollars in 2021. In addition, the major Internet giants have entered the market for market layout; Apple's Siri, Amazon's Alexa, Google's GoogleNow and Microsoft's Cortana have seized the smart home market. Due to the complexity of natural language and the large differences between different human speech, and the speech signal is easily disturbed by the environment, the accuracy of current Automatic Speech Recognition (ASR) is still not high enough.

In recent years, many researchers have done a lot of research on text correction for speech interaction scenarios. Back in 1997, Zhang and Wang [1] makes use of a hybrid statistical and rule approach to realize Chinese pinyin to text translation and puts forward an approach to correct some pinyin errors in the case of pinyin errors. In 2012, Bassil and Alwani [2] proposed a post-editing ASR error correction method and algorithm based on Bing's online spelling suggestion. Experiments carried out on various speeches in different languages indicated a successful decrease in the number

© Springer International Publishing AG, part of Springer Nature 2018
S. Liu et al. (Eds.): EDGE 2018, LNCS 10973, pp. 127–134, 2018.
https://doi.org/10.1007/978-3-319-94340-4_10

of ASR errors and an improvement in the overall error correction rate. In 2016, Fujiwara [3] designed a custom phonetic alphabet optimal for ASR. It enables the user to input words more accurately than spelling them out directly or using the NATO phonetic alphabet, which is known as the standardized phonetic alphabet used for human-human speech interaction under noise. Wang et al. [4] divided speech error correction process into four steps: (1) initial recognition; (2) detecting repeated words by computing the phonetic similarity between collected words and the CCN; (3) correcting recognition errors of repeated words automatically; (4) extracting new words from the recognition result of the current utterance.

In this paper, For the Chinese speech interaction context, we propose a POST-Editing Chinese text correction and intention recognition method for speech interaction. First of all, syntactic analysis of all the text material, extract the core components and use word2vec to extend the corpus, and then extract Pinyin to build inverted index. For the results after the ASR speech recognition, the Pinyin representation is extracted first, then the unvoiced sounds are unified, the retrieval is performed in the inverted index, and finally the distance is calculated using the improved edit distance.

2 Related Research

Pronunciation primitive: Chinese is a language composed of syllables. Syllables can be used as the basis for Chinese speech recognition. The internal structure of Chinese syllables is structured. Generally, each syllable can be divided into two parts: initials and finals [5]. It is a very good choice to use initials and finals as Chinese-specific pronunciation recognition primitives. Table 1 lists all Chinese initials and finals.

Table 1. Chinese initials and finals

Initials	b, p, m, f, d, t, n, l, g, k, h, j, q, x, zh, ch, sh, z, c, s, y, w, r
Simple finals	a, o, e, i, u, v
Compound finals	ai, ei, ui, ao, ou, iu, ie, ve, er, an, en, in, un, vn, ang, eng, ing, ong

Fuzzy tone: "Fuzzy tone" [6] is a pair of syllables that are easily confused and indistinguishable. Fuzzy tone is used most often in Pinyin input method. In the field of speech recognition, fuzzy tone is also useful, due to some Chinese pronunciation is very similar, brought a lot of trouble to speech recognition, using of fuzzy tones to unify all of these sounds is beneficial for the purpose of identification. Most of the fuzzy sounds are listed in Table 2.

Table 2. Fuzzy sound classification and statistics

Initials	(zh, z)(ch, c)(sh, s)(h, f)(r, l)
Finals	(ang, an)(eng, en)(ing, in)(iang, ian)(uang, uan)(ian, ie)
Overall	(fa, hua)(fan, huan)(fang, huang)(fei, hui)(fen, hun)(feng, hong)(fo, huo)(fu, hu)

3 The Framework of Speech Correction Overall Structure

This paper divides text correction and intention recognition of speech interaction context into two phases: corpus processing and text correction (Fig. 1).

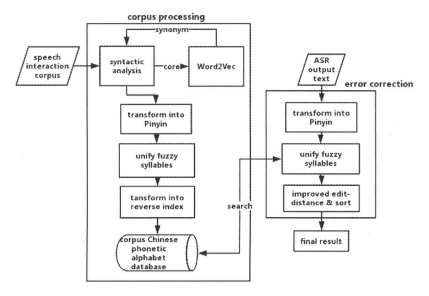

Fig. 1. Speech correction and intention recognition method for speech interaction context

At the corpus processing stage, firstly obtain the question and answer corpus of the required context, and then remove the colloquial stop words and then perform a sequential dependency analysis on these corpus. The main purpose is to extract the core components. These core component words can roughly express the overall meaning of the sentence. But because of the diversity of language, many words can express the same or similar, we use the Word2Vec model to replace the core components to generate more similar question and answer corpus and extend the usability of the model. Next, we will convert the generated linguistic data into Chinese Pinyin form, and establish an inverted index to help us to conduct fast retrieval and timely response.

In the text correcting stage, we first need to obtain text data from ASR, and then convert the text data into Chinese Pinyin, and then replace all the Pinyin with a unified fuzzy word, and query the n words whose edit distance is less than k in the inverted index. We use the improved edit distance method designed in this paper to perform distance calculations on these n words, and output the most likely text error correction and intent recognition results.

3.1   Speech Recognition Error Analysis

In ASR systems, textual errors can generally be divided into three types:

(1) The pronunciation is the same (similar) but the characters are different
Since the ASR system is essentially a model for sounds and characters (words), the model can often accurately recognize word sounds (or similar word sounds) but output wrong words. For Examples "登录金蝶云" (means login to Kingdee cloud) was identified as "登录经典云" (means login classic cloud") or "登录金典语言" (means login classic language). At this time, text correction is needed to replace the text with the correct representation.

(2) The meaning is the same (similar) but the characters are different
Due to the diversity of natural language, we usually have many ways to express the same thing, and the speech interaction is usually a language that is biased toward colloquialism, and contains many meaningless stop words (such as "让我" (means let me) and "一下" (means a bit). The presence or absence of a word does not affect the core meaning of the whole sentence. For example, we say that "运行人人绩效这个应用让我来看一看" (means Open this application "everyone's performance" let me take a look) to express the "打开人人绩效" (means open "everyone's performance") order. At this time, intention recognition is needed to identify the true intention.

(3) Mixed
This type is a mixture of the above two types. That is to say, the recognized text itself is wrong, and the semantics is also just an approximate representation of our linguistic problems. At this time, it is necessary to organically combine text correction and intention recognition.

3.2   Corpus Processing Stage

For a speech interaction application, corpus is needed as a support, the first is to train the speech recognition model, and the second is to define the ability range. We need to do some semantic extensions to support more comprehensive intent recognition, and we need to establish a suitable model to support sorting and distance calculations.

First, we analyze the corpus by dependency syntax to find the core components of the sentence. Dependency Parsing (DP) [7] reveals its syntactic structure by analyzing the dependencies between components within a linguistic unit. Intuitively speaking, grammatical components such as "subject-verb-object" and "attributive-adverbial-complement" are identified in a sentence-by-syntax analysis, and the relationships among the components are analyzed. For a sentence, the core component can roughly express the approximate meaning of the sentence, so the core component plays an extremely important role for a sentence. For the voice interaction scenario, the core component of the user's question is often a representative verb, such as "提出" (means propose), "打开" (means open), "播放" (means play) etc. These words are often highly substitutable, such as "播放" You can use "运行" instead.

Then, we use the trained Word2Vec [8, 9] to generate synonym words for the core words and replace the core words in the original sentences to generate new corpus. Word2Vec is a three-layer neural network model. It trains a large number of texts, and it can be used to vectorize the words very well. With additional data structures, synonyms can be calculated. The new corpus generated using the synonym to replace the core words is semantically the same as the previous sentences, which can expand the usability of intention recognition.

Then, all the corpus is converted into Pinyin representations and the fuzzy sounds are replaced. All the phonetic alphabets which have similar pronunciation are replaced by a single representation. After a unified replacement, the accuracy of speech recognition can be greatly improved.

Finally, all the Pinyin is built inverted index for storage. The inverted index can improve the efficiency of the fuzzy query, and the common inverted index engine can quickly perform the search of the specified edit distance range. This operation helps us to filter candidate results.

3.3   Error Correction Stage

For the text information t_0 output by the ASR system, since the speech input of the ASR is often spoken text, it is necessary that we need to preprocess it. The purpose of preprocessing is to remove all redundant characters and words on the premise of retaining as many core sentences as possible in order to keep the sentences streamlined so that we can perform algorithm analysis. The commonly used pre-processing method is to use the stop word list after the segmentation to filter out the stop words. In this paper we uses the stop words data set provided by the Hanlp project [10] to perform stop word culling operations. The dataset contains 1,208 Chinese and English stop words.

Similarly, after the text preprocessing, we also need to convert the text into a Chinese Pinyin form, and then unify the fuzzy word.

Next, we need to search in the reverse index database generated by the Corpus processing stage to get n pieces of corpus with the closest edit distance to t_0 for further analysis. This paper uses Solr [11] to construct the inverted index. Solr is a high-performance, full-text search server based on Lucene [12] developed by Java. It extends on the basis of Lucene, provides a richer query language than Lucene, and is configurable, extensible, and optimized for query performance. It is a very good full-text search engine. Solr helps us quickly build inverted indexes and can quickly perform distance-based searches. By querying Solr, we obtained n pieces of corpus which is nearest of t_0 in editing distance. In this way, we do not need to calculate the distance between t_0 and each corpus, which greatly reduces the system response time and load.

Next, we need to use t_0 and n pieces of acquired corpus $t_1 - t_n$ to calculate distances one by one to further narrow the candidate set. This paper uses a modified edit distance to perform this distance calculation.

The traditional editing distance has a problem with the speech interaction context. That is, if the lengths of the two strings differ greatly, the distance between the strings cannot be well represented.

In order to solve this problem, this paper improves the traditional editing distance algorithm. Improvements include the following:

(1) Pinyin texts are separated using the separator "-", which can avoid the appearance of Pinyin ambiguity and increase the editing distance between words.

(2) Introducing Pinyin Word Length Regular Terms:

$$lr = abs(len(t_0) - len(t_i)) \times \left(\sum_{w\ in\ t_0}^{w} len_p(w) + \sum_{w\ in\ t_i}^{w} len_p(w) \right) \bigg/ (len(t_0) + len(t_i))$$

The abs(x) method refers to the calculation of the absolute value of x, the len(x) method refers to the number of words of x, and the lenp(x) refers to the number of letters in Pinyin of x. Adding Pinyin word length regular terms to the Pinyin editing distance can better calculate the distance for texts with a large difference in length, which is more suitable for speech interaction contexts.

4   Experiments

In order to verify the effectiveness of our method in the Chinese speech interaction context, the method designed in this paper was connected to a smart ASR system, the validity test was conducted by the multi-person round-call question test method. Finally, the results were manually labeled. The test example is shown in Table 3.

Table 3. Test example

Correct use case	Examples that should be corrected
登录金蝶云(means login to Kingdee cloud)	登录今年人(means log in this year)、放首歌登陆金蝶云(means Putting the song on the landing of Kingdee cloud)、欧陆经典(meaningless)
解读一下吧(means read it)	请帮我解微笑吧(meaningless)、给我介绍一下吧(means tell me about it)、播放陈解读一下吧(meaningless)
查看深圳分公司 (means view Shenzhen branch)	看看深圳的走私(meaningless)、看看深圳怎么说(means see how Shenzhen says)、看看深圳有没有(means see if there is Shenzhen)

We can see that some of these ASR misidentification use cases are similar in pronunciation and some are semantically similar. We test on such a data set. The test results are shown in Table 4.

We can see that our method can greatly improve the accuracy of text recognition in ASR system. By analyzing the erroneous use cases, we found that in addition to invalid (i.e. meaningless) exceptions, errors can be categorized into the following categories:

Table 4. Test results

Total number of test cases	1189
Effective use cases	974
The correct number of ASR identifies	613
The correct number of ASR identifies + our method	836
Correct rate of ASR	62.9%
Correct rate of ASR + our method	85.8%

(1) Intentional identification failure. For example, "放频道霍金连云" should be identified as "放频道金蝶云" or "播放频道金蝶云" (means playing channel Kingdee cloud), but since corpus processing stage does not use the "play channel" as a synonym for the core word "open". Caused intention identification failure

(2) The input text is too long. Such as "小k你好，很高兴见到你，我现在想让你帮我运行人人绩效让我看看，好不好" (means hello little K, I'm very glad to meet you. I want you to help me run the "performance of everyone". Let me see if it's OK) Because the text is too long, it leads to a large deviation from the calculation. As a result, error correction fails.

(3) ASR is incomplete. Due to the ASR's own reasons or environmental reasons, the identified text is different from the real text, or it fails to recognize the integrity. For example, "登今年" (meaningless) we guessed that the speaker's intention was to "登录金蝶云" (means login to the Kingdee cloud) but due to missing some information, the error correction failed.

5   Conclusions

This paper first briefly introduces the industry development and research trends in the field of voice interaction, and points out the problems and deficiencies in text correcting and intention recognition. On this basis, the method of text error correction and intention recognition of the face-to-face speech interaction as described in this paper is proposed. The method uses semantics and speech to perform error correction. It is possible to deal with mixed complex contexts. Finally, a large number of tests are carried out using test cases. The experiment shows that the accuracy of ASR system can be greatly improved by the text error correction and intention recognition method.

But at the same time, we discovered some deficiencies in the system:

(1) Since the traditional edit distance algorithm is used in the search, the improved edit distance algorithm is used when the final result set is calculated. Therefore, the result set obtained in some cases is not the result we hoped for.

(2) Since all texts are unreliable and error-prone, the improved optimization method designed in this paper will fail at some point and does not have the desired effect. When the improvement method fails, it will degenerate into a Ordinary editing distance algorithm.

(3) Analyze the error use case to find that there is still room for further optimization in the intent recognition. The method in this paper is not effective in dealing with the long text and incomplete recognition.

Acknowledgement. This work is partially supported by the technical projects No. 2017YFB1 400604, No. 2016YFB1000803, No. 2017YFB0802703, No. 2012FU125Q09, No. 2015B010 131008 and No. JSGG20160331101809920.

References

1. Zhang, R., Wang, Z.: Chinese pinyin to text translation technique with error correction used for continuous speech recognition. J. Tsinghua Univ. (1997)
2. Bassil, Y., Alwani, M.: Post-editing error correction algorithm for speech recognition using bing spelling suggestion. Int. J. Adv. Comput. Sci. Appl. **3**(2) (2012)
3. Fujiwara, K.: Error correction of speech recognition by custom phonetic alphabet input for ultra-small devices. In: CHI Conference Extended Abstracts on Human Factors in Computing Systems, pp. 104–109. ACM (2016)
4. Wang, X., Li, X., Qian, Y., et al.: Automatic error correction for repeated words in Mandarin speech recognition. J. Autom. Control Eng. **4**(2), 153–158 (2016)
5. Yebo, B., Yu, H., Cong, L., et al.: Phoneme modeling units design for Mandarin LVCSR systems. J. Tsinghua Univ. (Science and Technology) **2011**(9), 1288–1292 (2011)
6. Qingqing, Z., Jielin, P.: The application of fuzzy pronunciation dictionary in dialect accent speech recognition. In: The 8th National Man-machine Speech Communication Conference Proceedings (2005)
7. Hall, J., Nilsson, J.: CoNLL-X shared task: multi-lingual dependency parsing. Matematiska Och Systemtekniska Institutionen (2006)
8. Mikolov, T., Sutskever, I., Chen, K., et al.: Distributed representations of words and phrases and their compositionality. In: International Conference on Neural Information Processing Systems, pp. 3111–3119. Curran Associates Inc. (2013)
9. Mikolov, T., Chen, K., Corrado, G., et al.: Efficient estimation of word representations in vector space. Comput. Sci. (2013)
10. Hanlp (2018). https://github.com/hankcs/HanLP
11. Apache. Solr (2018). http://lucene.apache.org/solr/
12. Apache. Lucene (2018). https://lucene.apache.org/

FCN-biLSTM Based VAT Invoice Recognition and Processing

Fei Jiang[1,2(✉)], Huan Chen[1,2], and Liang-Jie Zhang[1,2]

[1] National Engineering Research Center for Supporting Software of Enterprise Internet Services, Shenzhen, China
[2] Kingdee Research, Kingdee International Software Group Company Limited, Shenzhen, China
faye_jiang@kingdee.com

Abstract. Financial Sharing Centre of big or medium-sized enterprises that need to handle a large number of VAT invoices every day, but these invoices are often handled manually in poor efficiency. They need automation of unsupervised processing systems for VAT invoices to reduce costs and also to promote their financial management capability. In this paper, we develop FCN-biLSTMs that are capable of processing and recognizing invoice automatically. In view of the characteristics of invoice, we propose the methods that extract text lines by using invoice layout information and text characteristics, and achieve higher accuracy. Combined with the previous text detection methods and the attention-based biLSTM sequence learning structure for text recognizing, we developed an automatic VAT invoice recognition and processing system. The system in the actual projects of enterprises has achieved impressive performance.

Keywords: FCN · biLSTM · Invoice recognition and processing

1 Introduction

Chinese domestic value-added tax (VAT) invoice is an important accounting and billing document and is a corporate tax certificate, and it is widely present in dealings among enterprises. The format of it is under strict control of State Administration of Taxation. Financial Sharing Centre of big or medium-sized enterprises need to handle a large number of VAT invoices every day, but these invoices are often handled manually in poor efficiency. They need automation of unsupervised processing systems for VAT invoices to reduce costs and also to promote their financial management capability [1]. There are some projects of this kind that have been built or have been bringing forth to build. The undergoing of an enterprise internal ERP plans is providing a good infrastructure for it, and also, the developing of image processing technologies such as text detection, text recognition and others are coming into a state of commercial feasibility for it, with some extra efforts we can turn the VAT invoice image recognition and processing automation into reality.

Due to the large variability of text patterns and the highly complicated background, the recognition and processing for photo VAT invoice images are much more challenging than the scanned ones. An overview of the network architecture is presented in

© Springer International Publishing AG, part of Springer Nature 2018
S. Liu et al. (Eds.): EDGE 2018, LNCS 10973, pp. 135–143, 2018.
https://doi.org/10.1007/978-3-319-94340-4_11

Fig. 1. It consists of a number of convolutional layers, corner points of text bounding boxes, segmentation maps for text, and layout information for regressing the text box locations, encoder for embedding proposals of varying sizes to fixed-length vectors, and an attention-based Long Short-Term Memory (LSTM) decoder for word recognition. Via this framework, an automatic VAT invoice recognition and processing system is built and implemented.

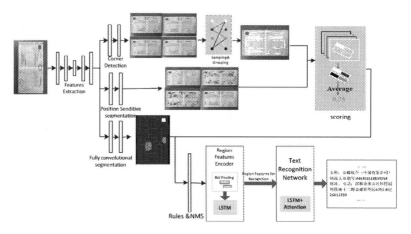

Fig. 1. Model overview. The network takes an image as input, and outputs both text bounding boxes and text labels.

We validate the effectiveness of our method on our accumulated VAT invoice image datasets in the enterprise financial management scenario. The results show the advantages of the proposed algorithm in accuracy and applicability.

The contributions of this paper are three-fold: (1) We propose a unified framework for processing and recognizing the VAT invoices, which can be trained and evaluated end-to-end. (2) Our method can simultaneously handle the challenges (such as rotation, varying aspect ratios, very close instances) in multi-oriented text in VAT invoice images. (3) We take invoice layout information into consideration and use some rule to regress and constrain the text bounding boxes.

2 Related Work

An automatic VAT invoice recognition and processing system essentially includes two tasks: text detection and word recognition. In this section, we present a brief introduction to related works on text detection, word recognition, and text spotting systems for VAT invoice that combine both. The text detection algorithm has developed rapidly in recent years. It can be roughly classified into two categories: horizontal text detection and skew text detection. For horizontal text detection, a number of approaches are proposed to detect words directly in the images using DNN based techniques, and it is similar to the method of object detection. Tian et al. [2] develop a vertical anchor mechanism, and propose a Connectionist Text Proposal Network (CTPN) to accurately localize text lines in image at ECCV 2016. The latest approach to skew text detection is SegLink [3] and Corner Localization and Region Segmentation proposed by Lyu [4]. SegLink [3] predicts text segments and the linkage of them in a SSD style network and links the segments to text boxes, in order to handle long oriented text in natural scene. Lyu et al. [4] propose to detect scene text by localizing corner points of text bounding boxes and segmenting text regions in relative positions. Word recognition has not made much progress in the last two years. There are two main methods, one of the methods is proposed by Shi et al. [5]. It is a novel neural network architecture, which integrates feature extraction, sequence modeling and transcription into a unified framework, while the another method is presented by Lee et al. [6] which use recursive recurrent neural networks with attention modeling for lexicon-free optical character recognition in natural scene images. Text spotting needs to handle both text detection and word recognition. Li et al. [7] proposed a unified network that simultaneously localizes and recognizes text with a single forward pass, avoiding intermediate processes like image cropping and feature re-calculation, word separation, or character grouping. Combining with specific application scenarios, Xie et al. [1] proposed to use many traditional images processing technology to develop the invoice automatic recognition and processing system.

3   Approach

3.1   Overall Architecture

The whole system architecture is illustrated in Fig. 1. It includes two parts: text detection network (TDN) and text recognition network (TRN). Text detection network aims to localize text in images and generate bounding boxes for words. Text recognition network recognizes words in the detected bounding boxes based on the previous text detection network. Our model is motivated by recent progresses in FPN [8], DSSD [9], Instance FCN models [10] and sequence-to-sequence learning [11, 12], and we also take the special characteristics of text and invoice layout information into consideration. In this section, we present a detailed description of the whole system.

3.2   Text Detection Network

The network of our method is a fully convolutional network (FCN) that plays the roles of feature extraction, corner detection, position-sensitive segmentation and fully convolutional segmentation. Inspired by the good performance achieved by FPN [8] and DSSD [9], we adopt the backbone in FPN/DSSD architecture to extract features. In detail, we convert the fc6 and fc7 in the VGG16 to convolutional layers and name them conv6 and conv7 respectively. Then several extra convolutional layers (conv8, conv9, conv10, conv11) are stacked above conv7 to enlarge the receptive fields of extracted features. After that, a few deconvolution modules proposed in DSSD [9] are used in a top-down pathway (Fig. 2). Particularly, to detect text with different sizes well, we cascade deconvolution modules with 256 channels from conv11 to conv3 (the features from conv10, conv9, conv8, conv7, conv4, conv3 are reused), and 6 deconvolution modules are built in total. Including the features of conv11, we name those output features F3, F4, F7, F8, F9, F10 and F11 for convenience. In the end, the feature extracted by conv11 and deconvolution modules, which have richer feature representations, are used to detect corner points and predict position-sensitive maps. A large number of candidate bounding boxes can be generated after sampling and grouping corner points. Inspired by [4], we adopt the methods which score the candidate boxes by Rotated Position-Sensitive Average ROI Pooling and detect the arbitrary-oriented text by using position-sensitive segmentation maps.

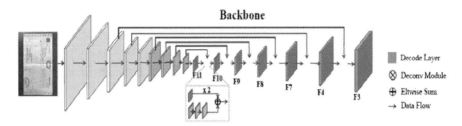

Fig. 2. Network architecture. The backbone is adapted from DSSD [9].

But unlike the above methods [4] that regress text boxes or segments directly, we still added the supplementary method, which uses the invoice layout information in the image (such as the form line, red chop and two-dimensional code.) detected by FCN architecture [13] to constrain the detected bounding boxes and to improve the accuracy and efficiency for text detection. Combine with the above method, we use the NMS and some rules to filter out the candidate boxes with low score and get the RoIs. The detected bounding boxes are merged via NMS according to their textness scores and fed into Text Recognition Network (TRN) for text recognition.

3.3   Text Recognition Network

To process RoIs of different scales and aspect ratios in a unified way, most existing works re-sample regions into fixed-size feature maps via pooling [14]. However, for text, this approach may lead to significant distortion due to the large variation of word lengths. For example, it may be unreasonable to encode short words like "Dr" and long words like "congratulations" into feature maps of the same size. In this work, we propose to re-sample regions according to their respective aspect ratios, and then use RNNs to encode the resulting feature maps of different lengths into fixed length vectors. The whole region feature encoding process is illustrated in Fig. 3.

For an RoI of size h × w, we perform spatial max-pooling with a resulting size of

$$H \times \min(W_{\max}, 2Hw/h), \tag{1}$$

where the expected height H is fixed and the width is adjusted to keep the aspect ratio as 2w/h (twice the original aspect ratio) unless it exceeds the maximum length W_{max}.

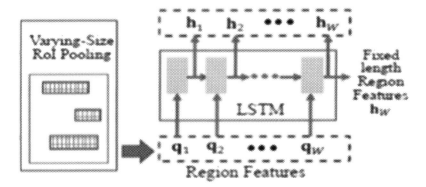

Fig. 3. Region Features Encoder (RFE). The region features after RoI pooling are not required to be of the same size. In contrast, they are calculated according to aspect ratio of each bounding box, with height normalized. LSTM is then employed to encode different length region features into the same size.

Note that here we employ a pooling window with an aspect ratio of 1:2, which benefits the recognition of narrow shaped characters, like 'i', 'l', etc., as stated in [5].

Next, the resampled feature maps are considered as a sequence and fed into RNNs for encoding. Here we use Long-Short Term Memory (LSTM) [11] instead of vanilla RNN to overcome the shortcoming of gradient vanishing or exploding. The feature maps after the above varying-size RoI pooling are denoted as $\mathbf{Q} \in \mathrm{R}^{C \times H \times W}$, where $W = \min(W_{max}, 2Hw/h)$ is the number of columns and C is the channel size. We flatten the features in each column, and obtain a sequence $\mathbf{q}_1, \ldots, \mathbf{q}_w \in \mathbf{R}^{C \times H}$ which are fed into LSTMs one by one. Each time LSTM units receive one column of feature $\mathbf{q}_t$, and update their hidden state $\mathbf{h}_t$ by a non-linear function: $\mathbf{h}_t = f(\mathbf{q}_t, \mathbf{h}_{t-1})$. In this recurrent fashion, the final hidden state $\mathbf{h}_W$ (with size $R = 1024$) captures the holistic information of Q and is used as a RoI representation with fixed dimension.

Text recognition aims to predict the text in the detected bounding boxes based on the extracted region features. As shown in Fig. 4, we adopt LSTMs with attention mechanism [12, 15] to decode the sequential features into words.

Firstly, hidden states at all steps $\mathbf{h}_1, \ldots, \mathbf{h}_W$ from RFE are fed into an additional layer of LSTM encoder with 1024 units. We record the hidden state at each time step and form a sequence of $\mathbf{V} = [\mathbf{v}_1, \ldots, \mathbf{v}_W] \in \mathbf{R}^{R \times W}$. It includes local information at each time step and works as the context for the attention model.

As for decoder LSTMs, the ground-truth word label is adopted as input during training. It can be regarded as a sequence of tokens $s = \{s0, s1, \ldots, s_{T+1}\}$ where s_0 and s_{T+1} represent the special tokens START and END respectively. We feed decoder LSTMs with $T + 2$ vectors: $x_0, x_1, \ldots, x_{T+1}$, where $x_0 = [\mathbf{v}_W; \mathrm{Atten}(\mathbf{V}, 0)]$ is the concatenation of the encoder's last hidden state v_W and the attention output with guidance equals to zero; and $x_i = [\psi(s_{i-1}; \mathrm{Atten}(\mathbf{V}, \mathbf{h}'_{i-1})]$, for $i = 1, \ldots, T+1$, is made up of the embedding $\psi()$ of the $(i-1)$-th token s_{i-1} and the attention output guided by the hidden state of decoder LSTMs in the previous time-step $\mathbf{h}'_{i-1}$. The embedding function $\psi()$ is defined as a linear layer followed by a tanh non-linearity.

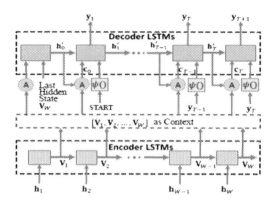

Fig. 4. Text Recognition Network (TRN). The region features are encoded by one layer of LSTMs, and then decoded in an attention based sequence to sequence manner. Hidden states of encoder at all time steps are reserved and used as context for attention model.

The attention function $c_i = \text{Atten}(V, h_i')$ is defined as follows:

$$\begin{cases} g_j = \tanh\left(W_v v_j + W_h h_i'\right), j = 1, \ldots, W, \\ \alpha = softmax\left(w_g^T \bullet [g_1, g_2 \ldots, g_w]\right), \\ c_i = \sum_{j=1}^{W} \alpha_j v_j \end{cases} \quad (2)$$

where $V = [v_1, \ldots, v_W]$ is the variable-length sequence of features to be attended, h_i' is the guidance vector, W_v and W_h are linear embedding weights to be learned, α is the attention weights of size W, and c_i is a weighted sum of input features.

At each time-step $t = 0, 1, \ldots, T + 1$, the decoder LSTMs compute their hidden state h_t' and output vector y_t as follows:

$$\begin{cases} h_t' = f(x_t, h_{t-1}') \\ y_t = \varphi\left(h_t'\right) = softmax(W_o h_t') \end{cases} \quad (3)$$

Where the LSTM [11] is used for the recurrence formula f(), and W_o linearly transforms hidden states to the output space, including 26 case-insensitive characters, 10 digits, common standard Chinese characters, a token representing all punctuations like "!" and "?", and a special END token.

At test time, the token with the highest probability in previous output y_t is selected as the input token at step t + 1, instead of the ground-truth tokens $s_1, \ldots, s_T$.

The process is started with the START token, and repeated until we get the special END token.

3.4   Loss Functions and Training

As we demonstrate above, our system takes as input of an image, word bounding boxes and their labels during training. For the final outputs of the whole system, we apply a multi-task loss for both detection and recognition.

$$L = L_D + L_R \tag{4}$$

Our text detect network model is trained by the corner detection and position-sensitive segmentation simultaneously. The loss function is defined as:

$$L_D = \frac{1}{N_c} L_{conf} + \frac{\lambda_1}{N_c} L_{loc} + \frac{\lambda_2}{N_s} L_{seg} \tag{5}$$

Where L_{conf} and L_{loc} are the loss functions of the score branch for predicting confidence score and the offset branch for localization in the module of corner point detection. L_{seg} is the loss function of position-sensitive segmentation. N_c is the number of positive default boxes, N_s is the number of pixels in segmentation maps. N_c and N_s are used to normalize the losses of corner point detection and segmentation. λ_1 and λ_2 are the balancing factors of the three tasks. In default, we set the λ_1 to 1 and λ_2 to 10.

We follow the strategy of text recognition which proposed by Lyu et al. [4] and the loss for training text recognition is.

$$L_R = \frac{1}{N_c} \sum_{i=1}^{N_c} L_{rec}(Y^{(i)}, s^{(i)}) \tag{6}$$

Where $s(i)$ is the ground-truth tokens for sample i and $Y_{(i)} = \left\{ y_0^{(i)}, y_1^{(i)}, \ldots, y_{T+1}^{(i)} \right\}$ is the corresponding output sequence of decoder LSTMs. $L_{rec}(Y, s) = -\sum_{t=1}^{T+1} \log y_t(s_t)$ denotes the cross entropy loss on $y_1, \ldots, y_{T+1}$, where $y_t(s_t)$ represents the predicted probability of the output being s_t at time step t and the loss on y_0 is ignored.

4   Experiments

In this section, we perform experiments to verify the effectiveness of the proposed method. We use the accumulated VAT invoice image datasets in the enterprise financial management scenario to evaluate the proposed method.

Our method is implemented by using TensorFlow r1.4.1. All the experiments are carried out on a workstation with an Intel Xeon 8-core CPU (2.10 GHz), 2 GeForce GTX 1080 Graphics Cards, and 64 GB RAM. Running on 1 GPUs in parallel, training a batch takes about 1 s. The whole training process takes less than a day.

For different application scenarios of the invoice, scanned invoices and photo invoices achieves different F-measures. The photo invoices is easily influenced by some factors such as size, noise, blur, illumination, contrast and shelter. One contribution of this work is added to the supplementary method,which uses the invoice layout information in the image to improve the accuracy and efficiency of text detection. To validate its effectiveness, we compare the performance of models "Ours FCN-biLATM+NoLayout" and "Ours FCN-biLATM+Layout". Experiment shows that the model with constrained layout rule significantly better than unconstrained layout rule. As illustrated in Tables 1 and 2, adopting constrained layout rule ("Ours FCN-biLATM +Layout") instead of unconstrained layout rule ("Ours FCN-biLATM+NoLayout") makes F-measures increase around 4%.

Table 1. Results on the scanned invoice image datasets. Precision (P) and Recall (R) at maximum F-measure (F) are reported in percentage.

Method	Precision	Recall	F-measure
Ours FCN-biLATM+NoLayout	89.0	83.0	66.0
Ours FCN-biLATM+Layout	93.3	79.4	85.8

Table 2. Results on the photo invoice image datasets. Precision (P) and Recall (R) at maximum F-measure (F) are reported in percentage.

Method	Precision	Recall	F-measure
Ours FCN-biLATM+NoLayout	66.0	44.7	53.3
Ours FCN-biLATM+Layout	70.8	43.0	53.6

5   Conclusion

In this paper, we have presented an automatic value-added tax (VAT) invoice recognition and processing system. In this system, VAT invoice can be detected and recognized in a single forward pass efficiently and accurately. Experimental results illustrate that the proposed method can produce an impressive performance in the actual projects of enterprises, and the model with constrained layout rule scenarios significantly better than unconstrained layout rule scenarios. One of potential future work is on maintaining images with other bills and documents.

Acknowledgement. This work is partially supported by the technical projects No. c1533411 500138 and No. 2017YFB0802700.

References

1. Xie, Z.G.: Researches on unsupervised image processing of VAT invoices, (Master Thesis) Shanghai Jiao Tong University, Shanghai, China (2015)
2. Tian, Z., Huang, W., He, T., He, P., Qiao, Yu.: Detecting text in natural image with connectionist text proposal network. In: Leibe, B., Matas, J., Sebe, N., Welling, M. (eds.) ECCV 2016. LNCS, vol. 9912, pp. 56–72. Springer, Cham (2016). https://doi.org/10.1007/978-3-319-46484-8_4
3. Shi, B., Bai, X., Belongie, S.: Detecting oriented text in natural images by linking segments. In: The IEEE Conference on Computer Vision and Pattern Recognition (CVPR), July 2017

4. Lyu, P., Yao, C., Wu, W., et al.: Multi-oriented scene text detection via corner localization and region segmentation. Journal (2018)

5. Shi, B., Bai, X., Yao, C.: An end-to-end trainable neural network for image-based sequence recognition and its application to scene text recognition. CoRR, abs/1507.05717 (2015)

6. Lee, C.Y., Osindero, S.: Recursive recurrent nets with attention modeling for OCR in the wild. In: Computer Vision and Pattern Recognition, pp. 2231–2239. IEEE (2016)

7. Li, H., Wang, P., Shen, C.: Towards end-to-end text spotting with convolutional recurrent neural networks. Journal (2017)

8. Lin, T.Y., Dollar, P., Girshick, R., He, K., Hariharan, B., Belongie, S.: Feature pyramid networks for object detection. In: The IEEE Conference on Computer Vision and Pattern Recognition (CVPR), July 2017

9. Fu, C.Y., Liu, W., Ranga, A., Tyagi, A., Berg, A.C.: DSSD: Deconvolutional single shot detector. arXiv preprint arXiv:1701.06659 (2017)

10. Dai, J., He, K., Li, Y., Ren, S., Sun, J.: Instance-sensitive fully convolutional networks. In: Leibe, B., Matas, J., Sebe, N., Welling, M. (eds.) ECCV 2016. LNCS, vol. 9910, pp. 534–549. Springer, Cham (2016). https://doi.org/10.1007/978-3-319-46466-4_32

11. Hochreiter, S., Schmidhuber, J.: Long short-term memory. Neural Comput. 9(8), 1735–1780 (1997)

12. Shi, B., Wang, X., Lv, P., Yao, C., Bai, X.: Robust scene text recognition with automatic rectification. In: Proceedings of the IEEE Conference on Computer Vision and Pattern Recognition (2016)

13. Long, J., Shelhamer, E., Darrell, T.: Fully convolutional networks for semantic segmentation. In: Proceedings of the IEEE Conference on Computer Vision and Pattern Recognition, pp. 3431–3440 (2015)

14. Girshick, R.: Fast R-CNN. In: Proceedings of the IEEE Conference on Computer Vision (2015)

15. Luong, M.T., Pham, H., Manning, C.D.: Effective approaches to attention-based neural machine translation. In: Proceedings of the 2015 Conference on Empirical Methods in Natural Language Processing (2015)

Research on Cross-Chain Technology
Based on Sidechain and Hash-Locking

Liping Deng[1,2(✉)], Huan Chen[1,2], Jing Zeng[1,2], and Liang-Jie Zhang[1,2]

[1] National Engineering Research Center for Supporting Software of Enterprise Internet Services,
Beijing, China
[2] Kingdee Research, Kingdee International Software Group Company Limited, Shenzhen, China
liping_deng@kingdee.com

Abstract. Blockchain is a distributed ledger, which includes public blockchains, private blockchains, and consortium blockchains. How to realize the exchange and transfer of value between different blockchains is an important research topic for the expansion of blockchain technology. This article describes what is cross-chain and elaborates the principles and cases of multi-signature wallet. Then it focuses on analyzing the current significant cross-chain technology and successful cross-chain projects. Finally, this article explores a new cross-chain solution.

Keywords: Cross-chain · Notary schemes · Sidechain · Relays · Hash-locking
Distributed private key control

1 Introduction

On October 31, 2008, Satoshi Nakamoto first proposed the concept of bitcoin in *Bitcoin: A Peer-to-Peer Electronic Cash System* [1], which opened up a new era of blockchain. Blockchain is a distributed ledger and a continuously growing list of records [2]. Currently, there are three types of blockchain networks: public blockchains, private blockchains and consortium blockchains. If the consensus mechanism is the soul of the blockchain, cross-chain technology is the key to realizing the value network for the blockchain, especially the consortium chain and the private chain. It is a good medicine to save the consortium chain from scattered and isolated islands. And it is a bridge to expand and connect blockchains [3]. From a business perspective, a blockchain is a value network. The more effective nodes that are connected, the wider the distribution, and the greater the resulting value stack. Blockchain is the core infrastructure of value network space. The application of blockchain cannot be confined to a single network.

In order to solve the trust mechanism between different blockchains and realize the information transmission between different blockchains, a cross-chain protocol is needed. The main contribution of this paper is to propose a cross-chain solution based on sidechain and hash-locking, thus constructing a value network highway.

The reminder of this paper is organized as follows: Sect. 2 introduces the related work about what is the cross-chain technology and multi-signature wallet. In Sect. 3, we present the existing cross-chain technology solutions, including Notary Schemes,

Sidechain/Relays, Hash-locking and Distributed Private Key Control. Section 4 introduces the current mature blockchain project on cross-chain technology, including Corda, Polkadot, Cosmos, and Wanchain. For Sect. 5, combined with Sidechain and Hash-locking technology, a solution for cross-chain blockchain technology is proposed.

2 Related Work

2.1 What Is Cross-Chain

The real society includes many industries and different economic fields. It is unrealistic to move the entire real world to a blockchain. Goods in different industries and different economic fields can realize value exchange through the market. Each blockchain is an independent value economic system. The cross-chain blockchain is the hub linking independent blockchains and carries the value exchange function of different value system blockchains. Price is the prerequisite for the exchange of goods. The price is determined by the value of the commodity itself and is influenced by the relationship between supply and demand, and the supply and demand relationship is built on the market. In order to realize the exchange of values on different blockchains, there will be various value transaction markets in the cross-chain blockchain. Each value transaction market in the cross-chain blockchain is a cross-chain contract service.

Cross-chain is a technology that allows value to cross the barrier between different blockchains and direct circulation [4]. Each blockchain is an independent ledger, two different blockchains correspond to two different independent ledgers, and there is no correlation between the two ledgers. In essence, value cannot be transferred between ledgers. However, for a specific user, the value stored in one blockchain can be translated into another blockchain value, which is the circulation of value.

Assuming Alice has 1 BTC and Bob has 12 ETHs, how can they trade? From the ledger point of view, the process of cross-chain operation is as follows (Table 1):

Table 1. Cross-chain operation process.

	Before transaction	Transaction	After transaction
Alice	1 BTC	Alice transfers 1 BTC to Bob	0
	0		12 ETHs
Bob	0	Bob transfers 12 ETH to Alice	1 BTC
	12 ETHs		0

To sum up, the core of cross-chain technology is to help user Alice on the Bitcoin blockchain to find Bob, the user who is willing to swap with the Ethernet blockchain. From a business perspective, cross-chain technology is an exchange that allows users to cross-chain transactions at the exchange.

Since Bitcoin and Ethereum belong to different blockchains, how do users between different blockchains establish trust mechanisms? If Alice transfers Bitcoin to Bob but Bob does not transfer Ethereum to Alice. So what should we do?

2.2 Multi-signature Wallet

In order to establish trust between Alice and Bob, trust transfer can be conducted through the trading platform. First, Alice transfers 1 BTC to the platform, and Bob transfers 12 ETHs to the platform. The trading platform then transferred 12 ETHs to Alice and 1 BTC to Bob. By holding a digital currency in the middle of the trading platform, the transfer of trust is realized, ensuring that Alice and Bob can perform cross-chain operations.

However, the trading platform must be credible? If he runs Alice's BTC and Bob's ETH. So what should we do? If the trading platform is operated by multiple entities, or is a public chain, anyone can participate in the operation of the trading platform. the risk of him running can be greatly reduced.

Using a multi-signature wallet allows multiple entities to jointly control an account [5]. In simple terms, multi-signature means that multiple users digitally sign the same message. In principle, A multi-signature address is an address that is associated with more than one ECDSA private key. The simplest type is an m-of-n address that is associated with n private keys, and sending bitcoins from this address requires signatures from at least m keys. A multi-signature transaction is one that sends funds from a multi-signature address.

Taking 2/3 multi-signature as an example, Alice, Bob, and the trading platform all have signing rights. If two of the principals confirm the signature, the transaction can proceed. Bob transfers 12 ETHs to a multi-signature address that is associated with a three-party private key. If the transaction is not going well, both Alice and Bob can arbitrate. After being investigated by the trading platform, they can decide whether to transfer ETH to Alice or return it to Bob through a signature.

3 Cross-Chain Technology

There are natural obstacles to the distribution of value between blockchains. Cross-chain is a complex process. It requires not only a separate verification capability for the nodes in the blockchain, but also a decentralized input, as well as the acquisition and verification of information outside the blockchain. Currently, cross-chain technologies mainly include: Notary schemes, Sidechain/Relays, Hash-locking and Distributed private key control.

3.1 Notary Schemes

The easiest way to interoperate between chains is to use the notary schemes [6]. In the notary mode, a trusted individual or group is used to declare to a blockchain that something has happened on another blockchain, or to make sure that the claim is correct. These groups can both automatically listen to and respond to events and listen and respond to events when they are requested.

Assuming that Alice and Bob can't trust each other, the third party that both Alice and Bob can trust is the intermediary of the notary. This establishes an indirect trust mechanism between Alice and Bob. The representative scheme is Interledger, which is not itself a ledger and does not seek any consensus. It provides a top-level encryption hosting system called "connectors", with the help of this intermediary, allowing funds to flow between ledgers.

3.2 Sidechain/Relays

The sidechain is not specifically referring to a blockchain, but refers to all blockchains that comply with the sidechain protocol and is a concept relative to the main chain of Bitcoin [7]. A sidechain protocol is an agreement that allows bitcoins to be safely transferred from the Bitcoin main chain to other blockchains, and that can be securely transferred back to the Bitcoin main chain from other blockchains [8]. The purpose of the sidechain protocol is to achieve two–way peg so Bitcoin can transit between the main chain and the sidechain. The sidechain protocol means Bitcoin can not only circulate on the Bitcoin blockchain, but also on other blockchains.

The essential feature of the sidechain/relay is to pay attention to the structure and consensus characteristics of the chain. In general, the main chain does not know the existence of the sidechain, but the sidechain must know the existence of the main chain; the double chain does not know the existence of the relay, but the relay must know the existence of the double chain.

3.3 Hash-Locking

Hash locking is a trigger that sets interoperation between different blockchains, usually a hash of the random number to be disclosed. It originated from Bitcoin's Lightning Network [9] and its key technology is the RSMC (Revocable Sequence Maturity Contract) and HTLC (Hashed Time Lock Contract).

Alice and Bob can reach a protocol: The protocol will lock Alice's BTC. Before time T, if Bob can show Alice an appropriate R, make R's hash value equal to the previously agreed value H(R), Bob can get this BTC; if at time T, Bob cannot provide a correct R, then this BTC will automatically thaw and return to Alice.

The use of hash locking can achieve the exchange of cross-chain assets, but can't achieve the transfer of cross-chain assets, but also can't achieve cross-chain contracts, its application scenario is more limited.

3.4 Distributed Private Key Control

The distributed private key control technology is a technology that uses a distributed private key generation and control technology to generate a locked account of the original chain and then maps the corresponding assets to its own blockchain. Wanchain and Fusion use this cross-chain technology. In this trading scheme, the account locking mechanism does not use a two-way peg method. All transaction data is transferred to the original chain node network after being reconstructed and synthesized at the verification node. This completely resolves the specific operations and calculations of the cross-chain transaction. Completed in the new blockchain, no need to modify any mechanism of the original chain, so that no matter existing public blockchains or private blockchains or consortium blockchains can freely access the blockchain, thus reducing cross-chain transactions Cooperative costs, to achieve free mapping of assets between the various chains.

4   Cross-Chain Project

At present, the research on cross-chain technology of blockchain is still in the exploratory stage. There are also some outstanding projects being tested. Below, we will focus on four cross-chain blockchain projects.

4.1   Corda

Corda is a blockchain platform created for the business world [10]. It eliminates the barriers between business transactions by achieving a direct exchange of business. Corda implements a collaborative, open network that gives companies greater ability to collaborate with each other and exchange value directly with one another.

Corda uses transactions to form a ledger, and its distributed ledger is an electronic record stored on all parties involved in a financial or commercial contract [11]. This information is stored in Corda Vault. At the same time, Corda will also store all trading histories, trace the history of a recorded matter and verify it independently.

Transactions in Corda are only spread between participants and notaries. The notary is chosen jointly by the parties to the transaction and is highly credible. The notary is responsible for verifying the validity of the data and verifying the uniqueness of the data. You can safely verify cross-billing messages by simply selecting cross-notices for different ledgers or forcing them to point to the same authenticator and synchronizing their ledgers.

4.2   Polkadot

Polkadot is a heterogeneous multi-chain technology [12]. It consists of many parachains with potentially differing characteristics which can make it easier to achieve anonymity or formal verification. Transactions can be spread out across the chains, allowing many more to be processed in the same period of time. Polkadot ensures that each of these blockchains remains secure and that any dealings between them are faithfully executed. Specialised parachains called bridges can be created to link independent chains.

Polkadot is a protocol that allows independent blockchains to exchange information. Polkadot is an inter-chain blockchain protocol which unlike internet messaging protocols (e.g. TCP/IP) also enforces the order and the validity of the messages between the chains. This interoperability also allows the additional benefit of scalability by creating a general environment for multiple state machines.

4.3 Cosmos

Cosmos is a decentralized network of independent parallel blockchains, each powered by classical BFT consensus algorithms like Tendermint [13]. The first blockchain in the Cosmos Network is the Cosmos Hub, whose native token is the Atom. Cosmos is a permissionless network, meaning that anybody can build a blockchain on it.

The Cosmos Center connects (or calls it space) many other blockchains through a new blockchain communication protocol. The center can track numerous token types and record the total number of tokens in each connected space. Tokens can be safely and quickly transferred from one space to another without the need to reflect exchange liquidity between the two, because the token transmission between all spaces passes through the Cosmos Center.

Cosmos is not just a single distributed ledger, but the Cosmos Center is not a closed garden or a cosmic center. We are designing a protocol for the open network of distributed ledgers. This protocol will become a new foundation for the future financial system based on the principles of encryption, robust economics, consensus theory, transparency, and accountability.

4.4 Wanchain

Wanchain is not merely a universal cross-chain protocol, it is a distributed ledger that records cross-chain and intra-chain transactions [14]. Wanchain connects and exchanges value between different blockchain ledgers in a distributed manner. It uses the latest cryptographic theories to build a non-proprietary cross-chain protocol and a distributed ledger that records both cross-chain and intra-chain transactions. Any blockchain network, whether a public, private or consortium chain, can integrate with Wanchain to establish connections between different ledgers and perform low cost inter-ledger asset transfers. The Wanchain ledger supports not only smart contracts, but also token exchange privacy protection.

When an unregistered asset is transferred from the original chain to Wanchain, Wanchain will create a new asset using a built-in asset template to deploy a new smart contract based on the cross-chain transaction information. When a registered asset is transferred from the original chain to Wanchain, Wanchain will issue the corresponding equivalent tokens in the existing contracts to ensure that the original chain assets can still be traded on Wanchain.

5   The Cross-Chain Solution

In the many problems faced by the blockchain, the network isolation hinders the cooperative operation between different blockchains, and limits the playing space of the blockchain to a great extent. In order to realize the information interaction between different blockchains, we explored a feasible scheme. The program combines side-chain technology and hash-locking technology to establish a new blockchain as a third-party trading platform, thus ensuring the transmission of trust between different blockchains.

The user develops a new blockchain as a trading platform. It can be either a public chain or a private chain for recording transaction credentials. The transaction credentials should appear in pairs, for which we have agreed on a trading interval, which is also the difference in the hash-locking interval. At the same time, the new blockchain can realize the quantification of value by issuing coins.

The specific implementation plan mainly includes three steps:

Step1: Both sides of the information exchange are registered as users on the new blockchain, and the corresponding wallet is opened. At the same time, it is necessary to deposit a sufficient amount of margin in personal accounts, which is a prerequisite for achieving cross-chain value transmission. Margin can be the new blockchain currency or other widely recognized and accepted cryptocurrencies such as BTC and ETH. As shown in Fig. 1, at t0, Alice and Bob each have an asset with a value of N as collateral. If Alice transfers assets to the Bob account on the chain A, there is no need to worry about Bob running away with the assets in the account.

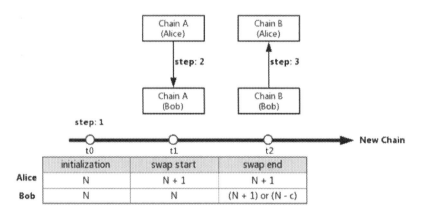

Fig. 1. A feasible cross-chain solution.

Step2: In order to encourage cross-chain transactions, all active parties based on the new blockchain will be rewarded. At t1, Alice and Bob make a transaction on block-chain A. The transaction initiator actively submits transaction credentials to the new blockchain. The blockchain records the transaction in real-time and issues a 1 unit bonus to Alice. After the record is complete, Alice's asset in the new block-chain account is N + 1 and Bob's asset is N.

Step3: In the case that the transaction is completed normally, at t2, on blockchain B, Bob will pay Alice's account the same amount of assets c as required by the prior agreement. After the transaction is complete, Bob submits the transaction credentials to the new blockchain, and Bob will also receive a bonus for 1 unit of assets. The cross-chain transaction was successfully implemented. If, after a given time interval, Bob still does not pay Alice the same amount of assets, or if the paid assets are less than the agreed value c. Bob will not be able to submit transaction credentials to the new blockchain normally. When the waiting time exceeds the hash-lock interval, Bob will deduct the same amount of assets c in the new blockchain account, meanwhile, the deducted assets c will pay for Alice as transaction compensation.

With the deepening of blockchain applications, cross-chain collaboration and inter-working between future blockchain systems is an inevitable trend. Cross-chain tech-nology is the key to the realization of value networks in blockchain, and the intercon-nection and interoperability of blockchains will become more and more important issues.

Acknowledgement. This work is partially supported by the technical projects No. 2016YFB1000803, No. 2017YFB0802703, No. 2017YFB1400604, No. 2012FU125Q09, No. 2015B010131008 and No. JSGG20160331101809920.

References

1. Nakamoto, S.: Bitcoin: a peer-to-peer electronic cash system. Consulted **1**, 28 (2008)
2. https://en.wikipedia.org/wiki/Blockchain. Accessed 8 May 2018
3. Gao, Z.: Blockchain cross-chain technology introduction. JKGC Mag. **11**, 46–51 (2016)
4. https://en.bitcoin.it/wiki/Atomic_cross-chain_trading. Accessed 10 May 2018
5. Yang, B., Chen, C.: The Principle, Design and Application of Blockchain, pp. 58–60. China Machine Press (2018)
6. https://www.jianshu.com/p/7dd5305d71b6. Accessed 10 May 2018
7. Chang, J., Han, F.: Blockchain from Digital Currency to Credit Society, pp. 84–87. China CITIC Press (2016)
8. Back, A., Corallo, M., Dashjr, L., Friedenbach, M., Maxwell, G., Miller, A., Poelstra, A., Timón, J., Wuille, P.: Enabling blockchain innovations with pegged sidechains. https://blockstream.com/sidechains.pdf
9. Poon, J., Dryja, T.: The bitcoin lightning network: scalable off-chain instant payments. https://lightning.network/lightning-network-paper.pdf
10. http://cncorda.com/. Accessed 10 May 2018
11. Hearn, M.: Corda: a distributed ledger. https://docs.corda.net/_static/corda-technical-whitepaper.pdf
12. Wood, G.: Pounder. Polkadot: Vision for a Heterogeneous Multi-chain Framework. https://block.academy/researches/PolkaDotPaper.pdf
13. Kwon, J., Buchman, E.: Cosmos: a network of distributed ledgers. https://cosmos.network/resources/whitepaper
14. Wanchain: Building Super Financial Markets for the New Digital Economy. https://www.wanchain.org/files/Wanchain-Whitepaper-EN-version.pdf

Author Index

Printed in the United States
By Bookmasters